J. Krishnamurti expounded original ideas on subjects such as freedom, truth, fear, death and purpose of life.

Here is an exploration into the life and message of this remarkable man, an enigma who offered no nostrums or techniques for spiritual growth, but who believed that we need to find out for ourselves where reality is.

KRISHNAMURTI
The Man, The Mystery & The Message

STUART HOLROYD

New Age Books

ISBN: 81-7822-268-x

First Indian Edition: Delhi, 2006

First published in Great Britain by Element Books Limited 1991
First published in the USA by Element Inc 1991

© Stuart Holroyd, 1991

All rights reserved. No part of this publication may be reproduced or transmitted in any form or by any means, electronic or mechanical, including photocopying, recording, or by any information storage and retrieval system, without permission in writing from the publishers.

Published with permission from Krishnamurti Foundation Trust.
More information on Schools, Foundations and Retreat Centres worldwide can be obtained by contacting: Krishnamurti Foundation Trust Brockwood Park, Bramdean, Hampshire, SO24 0LQ England
E-mail: info@brockwood.org.uk
Website: www.kfoundation.org.uk

Published by
NEW AGE BOOKS
A-44 Naraina Phase-I
New Delhi-110 028 (INDIA)
Email: nab@vsnl.in
Website: www.newagebooksindia.com

For Sale in Indian Subcontinent Only

Printed in India
at Shri Jainendra Press
A-45 Naraina Phase-I, New Delhi-110 028

Contents

Introduction 1

PART ONE: *The Man and The Mystery* 3

1. The Marvellous Boy 4
2. The Process 10
3. The Coming Gone Wrong 16
4. Exploring the Pathless Land 24
5. 'The Flowering' 34
6. The Poet of Awareness 42
7. The Mystery 49

PART TWO: *The Message* 59

8. On Human Bondage 60
9. On Mind, Consciousness and the Self 68
10. On Religion and the Religious Life 80
11. On Life and Death 91
12. The Psychological Revolution 100

PART THREE: *Developments and Applications* 109

13. Living and Learning 110
14. Life's Problems 121
15. Science and the Future: the Bohm Dialogues ... 136

Appendix: Bohm's *Wholeness and the Implicate Order* ... 152
Bibliography 157
Index of Names and Places 159
Subject index 161

Acknowledgements

Nobody can write about Krishnamurti without being profoundly indebted to the three volumes of biography by his friend Mary Lutyens. *Krishnamurti: The Years of Awakening, Krishnamurti: The Years of Fulfilment,* and the moving account of his last years, *The Open Door,* constitute the definitive biography, and I am grateful to Mary Lutyens and to her publishers John Murray Ltd. for their permission to quote from these books.

The Trustees of the Krishnamurti Foundation Trust, Brockwood Park, Bramdean, Hampshire, England, have been most helpful and encouraging, and I thank them for permission to quote freely from Krishnamurti's published writings, talks and dialogues of which they hold the copyright, in particular *The Ending of Time* and *The Future of Humanity,* which Chapter 15 heavily relies upon, both in direct quotation and in paraphrase. The Foundation also generously furnished photographs of Krishnamurti, and the publishers join me in thanking them for this.

I thank Pupul Jayakar and her publishers Harper and Row Inc. for permission to quote from her biography, *Krishnamurti,* an invaluable account of Krishnamurti's visits to India and his work there.

I thank the Krishnamurti Foundation of America, holders of the copyright of *The First and Last Freedom,* the three *Commentaries on Living* volumes, and *This Matter of Culture,* for their permission to quote from these books.

I thank David Bohm for permission to quote and paraphrase material from his dialogues with Krishnamurti, published in *The Ending of Time* and *The Future of Humanity,* and also from his own book, *Wholeness and the Implicate Order.*

Finally, my thanks to Chetana Ltd. of Bombay for permission to quote from books by and about Krishnamurti, as listed in the Bibliography.

Introduction

In library catalogues Krishnamurti is generally listed as a philosopher. He would have demurred at the title, and few academic philosophers would have applied it to him, if only because he had read none of their books. In fact he professed to have read hardly anything, except thrillers and P. G. Wodehouse novels for entertainment, and in all his work there is scarcely a reference to any other writer. Yet what else do you call a man who, for more than half a century, explored and discussed such subjects as freedom, truth, fear, death, suffering, ethics, the purpose of life and the nature of intelligence? These are some of the perennial subjects of philosophy, and Krishnamurti expounded original ideas on all of them; ideas derived entirely from his own life experience.

What an extraordinary life experience it was; so extraordinary indeed that the teaching that emerged from it is perhaps too demanding and austere for the majority of people. In 1929 he declared it his purpose in life 'to set man free'. His prescriptions for the attainment of freedom and the conquest of fear and suffering are simple to comprehend, but for most people difficult in the extreme to practise. His ideal of the human condition was that described in the lines of the poet T. S. Eliot:

> A condition of complete simplicity
> Costing not less than everything.

Krishnamurti himself was prepared to pay the cost, and in his early life he was quite singularly situated to be able to do so, being provided for and protected from the harsher realities and the beguiling temptations of life in a manner befitting the young god that he was believed by many to be. His mode of life and a temperamental tendency towards mysticism combined to give him a number of religious experiences which at once enhanced his authority with his following and, paradoxically, caused him to repudiate that following. These experiences also served to lay the foundation of his philosophy.

Krishnamurti expounded this philosophy, in books and talks for some seventy years, and its lucid and challenging concepts have come to the notice of millions. If he had accomplished his declared aim, human beings would be fundamentally changed; so some may say that the aim was misconceived by a young man who was naïve to certain realities of life and human nature. But if he was not a world-changer he was certainly a world-influencer. Although he declared himself 'rather allergic to gurus', and insisted that nobody could learn anything of significance from anybody else, his patent distinction as a human being and a philosopher was such that over some three or four generations young people flocked to listen to him. When he died in 1986 his world-wide influence was certainly more profound than that of more flamboyant and well-publicized guru-figures who emanated from points East in the 1960s and 70s, who generally were in the business of marketing some nostrum or technique for the alleviation of human malaise and the attainment of that spiritual growth that all but the most benighted of human beings come to conceive as the purpose of life. Krishnamurti had no nostrums or techniques to sell, or even to recommend. Philosophy, he said, 'means the love of truth, not love of words, not love of ideas, not love of speculations, but love of truth. And that means you have to find out for yourself where reality is.'[1]*

Let us begin, then, by seeing how this remarkable man found out for himself 'where reality is'.

---

* The superscript numbers refer to books listed in the Bibliography on page 157.

PART ONE

•

The Man and The Mystery

I

The Marvellous Boy

It was a central belief in Theosophy, a religious movement established in 1875 by an American spiritualist, Colonel Olcott, and an energetic Russian emigré and occultist, Madame Helena Blavatsky, that at certain critical junctures in the history of the world a wonderfully wise and benevolent supernatural Being, the Lord Maitreya, had incarnated on earth in human form. Once, he had incarnated in India as Sri Krishna, and on another occasion in Palestine as Jesus Christ. Theosophists further believed that the time when the Lord Maitreya, the World Teacher, would become incarnate again was imminent, and Madame Blavatsky sometimes said that the main purpose of the Theosophical Society was to prepare mankind for the coming of the World Teacher. This theme was taken up after her death in 1891 by another Theosophist, Annie Besant, who later was to become President of the Society and to have what she considered the singular honour of being responsible for the upbringing of the World Teacher.

The actual discovery of the human being who was to embody the Lord Maitreya was made by another remarkable Theosophist, a former pupil of Madame Blavatsky named Charles Leadbeater. One day in the spring of 1909 Leadbeater, who reputedly had highly developed psychic and clairvoyant powers, saw a group of Indian children bathing on the beach at Adyar near Madras, where the headquarters of the Theosophical Society was situated. He observed to a friend that one of these children had an aura of quite extraordinary size and beauty, indeed one which indicated that he would become a great spiritual teacher and speaker. The friend, who said that he knew the boy because he had helped him with his homework, was astonished, for he had found him extremely dim-witted. The boy was one of the four surviving children (the eighth born out of thirteen) of an impoverished Brahmin widower named Narianiah, who had a humble post working for the Society and lived in appalling conditions in a hovel of a cottage outside the compound. He was a weak, undernourished-looking child aged fourteen, who was always in trouble at school for being vacant and inattentive, and it certainly redounds to the credit of Leadbeater's powers of psychic perception that this unlikely boy should turn out to be the great spiritual teacher and speaker Jiddu Krishnamurti.

The fact that he did so turn out, however, is partly attributable to Leadbeater's discovering him, and to the way that he and Mrs Besant brought him up, together with his brother Nitya. Narianiah, who was himself a Theosophist, was at first delighted that the leaders of the Society should interest themselves in the education of his boys. He was somewhat concerned about Leadbeater, who had a reputation for homosexuality, but he readily signed a document making Mrs Besant the boys' legal guardian. They were educated at Adyar, then later in England, and in addition to general subjects were given instruction in the principles of Theosophy. These were said to express the 'ancient wisdom', or corpus of occult knowledge of the mysteries of nature and the latent powers of man, disclosed to Madame Blavatsky and expounded in her books, and were believed to constitute the foundations of a 'Universal Brotherhood of Humanity' of which the Theosophical Society was the nucleus. Leadbeater and Mrs Besant soon decided that Krishnamurti was to be the 'vehicle' for the new incarnation of the Lord Maitreya, and that their task was to prepare him for this role. He learnt all about the Masters, those supernatural all-wise and all-loving Beings whom initiated Theosophists claimed to be able to visit by means of astral travel, and he himself, under Leadbeater's tutelage, paid astral visits to and received instruction from a certain Master Kuthumi. His first publication was an account of the teaching he received in this way and was titled *At the Feet of the Master*. It appeared just twenty months after the virtually illiterate boy had been discovered. In its first year it went through five English and twenty-two foreign-language editions, and remains in print to this day. At the time Leadbeater's secretary, Ernest Wood, remarked that: 'It was very much in Mr Leadbeater's own style, and there were some sentences that were exactly the same as in a book of his which we had already prepared for the press.'[39] The 'vehicle' himself was reported to have told his father, 'The book is not mine; they fathered it upon me',[39] but the statement was made in private and when it came to Mrs Besant's notice the person who reported having overheard it was promptly expelled from the Theosophical Society estate.

Another of Leadbeater's alleged psychic endowments was the ability to divine past lives. In 1910 he started publishing in *The Theosophist* his 'Lives of Alcyone', which were accounts of thirty previous incarnations of the boy Krishnamurti. His investigations revealed that the leading personalities in the Theosophical Society had worked together in previous eras, between the years 22,662 BC and AD 624, and that there was an ancient prophecy that the Lord Maitreya would take possession of the body of Alcyone in order to bring his blessing upon the world. These revelations caused some friction among Theosophists, who vied with each other to identify themselves with the pseudonyms in the 'Lives' and to claim past-life intimacy with the near-divine Alcyone.

Krishnamurti had always been a sensitive and religiously disposed child. After the death of his mother, when he was ten years old, he reported several times seeing her spirit engaged in activities around the house. On 11 and 12 January 1910 he underwent his 'First Initiation', a ceremony organized by Leadbeater at a supposedly astrologically propitious time. In an account of it which he wrote to Mrs Besant, Krishnamurti told how he had left his body and gone into the company of the Masters, among them the Lord Maitreya and the Master Jesus, who had asked him a number of questions before solemnly admitting him to the brotherhood of eternal life and giving him the key of knowledge. His report of the experience is very vivid, but whether it was an experience attributable to his psychic development or to his suggestibility must remain a moot point. What is significant is that the young Krishnamurti was clearly thoroughly indoctrinated with Theosophy and was convinced of his own extraordinary destined role, for some of the key themes that he later developed are clearly a strong reaction against this indoctrination and conviction.

On the first anniversary of Krishnamurti's 'Initiation' a prominent Theosophist named George Arundale formed an organization called the Order of the Rising Sun, dedicated to the single purpose of preparing the way for the ministry of the World Teacher. Some months later the organization was renamed the Order of the Star in the East and Krishnamurti was nominated the head of the Order. On 28 December 1911 there was an occurrence that convinced many of the boy's divinity. A ceremony was held at Benares, during which Krishnamurti was to give certificates of membership to people who had recently joined the Order. The procedure was not ritualized or charged with great religious significance. Members simply filed past the head of the Order, who smiled and said a word of welcome to them as he handed them their papers. But suddenly the atmosphere changed so dramatically that the member approaching Krishnamurti at the time involuntarily dropped to his knees and bowed his head to the ground. An observer wrote:

> All saw the young figure draw itself up and take on an air of serene and dignified majesty, a stateliness new and strange... A great coronet of brilliant shimmering blue appeared a foot or so above the young head, and from this descended, funnel-wise, bright streams of blue light, till they touched the dark hair, entering and flooding the head; the Lord Maitreya was there, embodying Himself in His Chosen.[32]

The written accounts of other witnesses of the scene are similarly ecstatic, and all tell how Krishnamurti laid his hands in blessing upon the new members, bestowing upon them a smile of extraordinary radiance, tenderness and compassion. Leadbeater wrote that 'It was exactly the kind of thing that we read about in the old scriptures, and think exaggerated',[32] and compared it with the biblical account of the descent of the Holy Spirit at Pentecost. Subsequently 28 December was regarded as a sacred day by members of the Order of the Star in the East.

Earlier in 1911 Mrs Besant had taken Krishnamurti and Nitya to Europe for the first time to begin their education. She travelled around giving a series of public lectures on 'The Coming of the World Teacher' and introducing 'Alcyone' to Theosophists. The Society had a number of wealthy and socially prominent members in England, and the two Indian boys were now given quite a different initiation than the one Krishnamurti had undergone with Leadbeater: an initiation into the rituals and amusements of the English aristocracy. Despite Leadbeater's reverence for the exotically named Beings of the Occult Hierarchy, he remained a typical Englishman of his day in believing that the pinnacle of human evolution was the English gentleman; accordingly the boys were privately tutored and their names were put down for places at Balliol College, Oxford, for the autumn of 1914.

After a brief return to India at the end of 1911, during which the above-related 'visitation' occurred, Mrs Besant rushed her charges back to Europe in order to get them away from their father, who was now threatening to have recourse to law to revoke Mrs Besant's guardianship. He maintained that there had been a verbal agreement that the guardianship was conditional on their having no contact whatsoever with Leadbeater, and that this condition had not been complied with. He eventually brought an action in the High Court of Madras in March 1913, alleging an improper relationship between Leadbeater and the boys. After protracted hearings of evidence, the Judge ordered that Krishnamurti and Nitya should be made Wards of Court, which meant that they would have to return to India. Mrs Besant appealed against the decision, arguing that it would be against the boys' best interests to deprive them of the education that they were embarked upon, but the Appeal Court upheld the judgement of the lower court. A less determined person would have submitted at this point, but Mrs Besant took her appeal to the Judicial Committee of the Privy Council in London, who ruled that as the boys' wishes had not been consulted by the Madras Court its judgement was misconceived, and pointed out that if Mrs Besant had obeyed the Court's order she would have contravened the law of England by taking the boys out of the country against their will. The Committee ascertained that the boys did not wish to return to India, and dismissed Narianiah's suit.

Leadbeater's and Mrs Besant's intention of having their protégés educated at Britain's most august university was thwarted, partly on account of the publicity given to the Court proceedings, but also no doubt because no Oxford college was keen to have among its alumni a young man who had been proclaimed a kind of Messiah. The universities of Cambridge and London were equally circumspect, and the brothers continued to receive most of their education from private tutors. Nitya managed to pass his matriculation examinations and eventually to qualify as a barrister but Krishnamurti twice failed the examinations, which, however, did not prevent him from attending lectures at London University as an external student during the years 1917–18. In later life he often said that he was glad that his mind had not been conditioned by a formal academic education, but in youth he did his utmost to fulfil Mrs Besant's plans for him, and was disappointed by his academic failures.

While he was pursuing his studies, Krishnamurti continued as head of the Order of the Star and wrote regular editorials for the Order's magazine, the *Herald of the Star*. These were orthodox Theosophical tracts, sustaining readers' faith in the coming of the

World Teacher and urging and guiding their personal spiritual preparation for the great event. By the early 1920s the Order had more than 30,000 members, and in 1921 some 2000 of them attended a Congress in Paris, at which Krishnamurti spoke. He was now twenty-six years old, and was developing authority in his role. Mrs Besant wrote that on this occasion 'he astonished all present by his grasp of the questions considered, his firmness in controlling the discussions, his clear laying down of the principles and practices of the Order.'[32]

One principle which he laid down particularly emphatically was that there should be no rituals in the Order of the Star. It was the first sign of his repugnance to all the pomp and mumbo-jumbo through which many religious leaders in the past had sought to buttress their authority. It was also, perhaps, a gesture of independence from Leadbeater, who loved ceremonial and dressing up in sacerdotal garb, although Krishnamurti was not at this stage becoming sceptical of the organization and purposes of Theosophy. After attending a session of the League of Nations at Geneva, he wrote to a friend criticizing the insincerity and superficiality of the delegates, and said, 'I know how much better we Theosophists could manage the League of Nations, for I think we are more disinterested. You wait, when we get going we shall make a hum and beat them all at their own game.'[32]

The youthful combativeness and confidence of this is engaging, if scarcely consistent with the image of the budding World Teacher of surpassing wisdom. And likewise inconsistent with that image are several expressions of self-doubt and uncertainty which he put in letters to friends written at this time. For instance, he wrote to Lady Emily Lutyens: 'I do a vague kind of meditation, but I must do it more rigorously and regularly. That's the only way. I don't know the philosophy of my life, but I *will* have one... I must find myself and then *only* can I help others.'[32] Clearly something quite exceptional had to happen to turn this man of twenty-six, with his sheltered background and with all the normal confusions and inner conflicts of a sensitive and intelligent person of that age, into an authoritative World Teacher, or even into the lucid and positive philosopher that Krishnamurti was to become.

2
The Process

SOMETHING did happen, in August 1922, at Ojai in California. Krishnamurti later called it 'the process' and regarded it as the turning-point in his life. He arrived with Nitya in California from the West, after travelling from Europe over a period of several months and attending Theosophical Conventions in India and Australia. There they had spent time with Leadbeater, who now boasted the title of Regionary Bishop for Australasia of the Liberal Catholic Church, a post which enabled him to indulge his taste for flamboyance and ceremonial. Leadbeater had 'brought through' for Krishnamurti a message from the Master Kuthumi which had a profound effect upon him. The message went:

> Of you, too, we have the highest hopes. Steady and widen yourself, and strive more and more to bring the mind and brain into subservience to the true Self within. Be tolerant of divergencies of view and method, for each has usually a fragment of truth concealed somewhere within it, even though oftentimes it is distorted almost beyond recognition. Seek for the tiniest gleam of light amid the Stygian darkness of each ignorant mind, for by recognising and fostering it you may help a baby brother.[32]

Platitudinous though it was, this message seemed to Krishnamurti very relevant to his condition at the time. 'As you know', he wrote to Leadbeater,

> I have not been what is called 'happy' for many years; everything I touched brought me discontent. . . I did not know what I wanted to do nor did I care to do much; everything bored me in a very short

time and, in fact, I did not find myself.'

As a result of the message that he believed to emanate from Master Kuthumi he began to meditate regularly, and a consequence of his meditation was, he wrote, that 'I began to see clearly where I had failed and where I was failing and...began consciously and deliberately to destroy the wrong accumulations of the past years.'[32]

But 'the process' was not a deliberate intellectual assessment of himself and his life; it was an overwhelming physical and spiritual experience.

In his classic study, *Shamanism*, Mircea Eliade tells how the shaman of primitive tribal religions was often 'a sick man who had succeeded in curing himself', and says that often the shaman's vocation was first revealed 'through an illness or epileptoid attack'. Furthermore, a characteristic of this revelatory illness is that the shaman experiences a separation from his physical body, and goes into a trance 'during which his soul is believed to leave his body and ascend to the sky or descend to the underworld'. These quotations are remarkably descriptive of what happened to Krishnamurti.

Both Krishnamurti and Nitya wrote accounts, and the two are complementary, the former giving a subjective view and the latter an objective one.

They had been staying at Ojai, about eighty miles north of Los Angeles, for some six weeks. Nitya described Ojai at that time as a secluded and idyllic place, a narrow valley of apricot orchards and orange groves. It was through the general secretary of the Theosophical Society in America, A. P. Warrington, that the brothers had been given the use of a cottage in the valley. Warrington himself was staying at another cottage nearby. The reason for their stay was that Nitya had for some time been suffering from tuberculosis, and the climate at Ojai was said to be very beneficial for this condition. For part of their stay they had a pretty nineteen-year-old American girl, named Rosalind Williams, to look after Nitya. She and Warrington both witnessed what happened to Krishnamurti.

It started one evening when Krishnamurti developed a painful lump in the middle of the nape of his neck. The next morning he was found tossing and moaning on his bed as if in great pain. Rosalind would hold him for a while, which calmed him, but then he would suddenly push her away, complaining of terrible heat. He went on like this all day, with brief periods of calm and lucidity. He could eat no food. After a fairly tranquil night the same condition continued in a more acute form all through the next day, which was a Saturday. On the Sunday he was even worse, showing little control of the trembling that shook his body, becoming conscious only intermittently and briefly, continually talking to people who were not there, and reacting hypersensitively to the slightest sounds.

The condition came to a climax on the Sunday evening. Just after the others had finished their evening meal, wrote Nitya, 'suddenly the whole house seemed full of a terrible force and Krishna was as if possessed'. He sobbed aloud, would have nobody near him, and complained vehemently about everything being dirty. At his urging, the others left the room and went out onto the verandah, where he presently joined them, but sat as far away as possible on a cushion on the floor, murmuring incoherently. Then, prompted by a suggestion from Warrington, he went and sat under a pepper tree just in front of the house, and there, after a time, he began to chant a mantram. The scene reminded Nitya of the story of the Buddha's illumination under the Bo tree. All three witnesses strongly felt that in these moments Krishnamurti was visited by a Presence. 'The place seemed to be filled with a great Presence,' wrote Nitya, 'and a great longing came upon me to go on my knees and adore, for I knew that the Great Lord of all our hearts had come Himself.'[32] Rosalind, although she had no background in Theosophy, spoke of actually seeing the Lord Maitreya, accompanied by other radiant beings: a vision which lasted about half an hour, after which she fell into a swoon. Krishnamurti remained under the pepper tree all that night and the next day. On the evening of that day Rosalind saw three figures appear and take him away, leaving his physical body under the tree.

So goes Nitya's account. Krishnamurti's own account of the experience of those three days relates the same sequence of events, and culminates with a paean of celebration of the visionary experience he had sitting under the pepper tree:

> When I had sat thus for some time, I felt myself going out of my body, I saw myself sitting down with the delicate tender leaves of the tree over me. I was facing the east. In front of me was my body and over my head I saw the Star, bright and clear. Then I could feel the vibrations of the Lord Buddha; I beheld the Lord Maitreya and Master K. H. [Kuthumi]. I was so happy, calm and at peace . . . The Presence of the mighty Beings was with me for some time and then

They were gone. I was supremely happy, for I had seen. Nothing could ever be the same. I had drunk of the clear and pure waters at the source of the fountain of life and my thirst was appeased. Never more could I be thirsty, never more could I be in utter darkness; I have seen the glorious and healing Light. The fountain of truth has been revealed to me and the darkness has been dispersed. Love in all its glory has intoxicated my heart; my heart can never be closed. I have drunk at the fountain of Joy and Beauty. I am God-intoxicated.[32]

Krishnamurti later wrote to Leadbeater that after this experience he knew what he wanted to do and what lay before him – 'nothing but to serve the Masters and the Lord'. To his chief correspondent and closest friend Lady Emily Lutyens, he wrote: 'I am going to help the whole world climb a little higher than they are,' and he urged her to 'change, change with deliberation and a set purpose,' apologizing for seeming to preach, but explaining that 'since I have changed and now that I consider that I have found myself, I want to help you realise your own self and to become great.'[32] And in these words he stated the fundamental purpose to which all his writing and talking over the next half century would be dedicated, though of course not in regard to Lady Emily alone but for anyone who cared to listen to him.

It was generally believed among Theosophists that Krishnamurti's 'process' was, as Leadbeater put it, 'the preparation of that body for its Great Occupant'. The experience was not confined to those three days in August 1922 at Ojai, but was recurrent over the next eighteen months. During this period Krishnamurti travelled a great deal addressing gatherings of Theosophists, which he did with increasing assurance and authority. Although 'the process' caused him very great physical suffering, he did not once consider consulting a doctor about it, for he construed it in terms of the traditional concepts of Yoga philosophy and occult anatomy, according to which the process of evolution is accomplished through the opening or awakening of different *chakras*, or force centres, in the body, notably the *kundalini* centre at the base of the spine.

In August and September 1923, after a strenuous time presiding over the second international Star Congress in Vienna, Krishnamurti spent some weeks relaxing in a village in the Alps, near Innsbruck, with a party of friends, which included Lady Emily Lutyens and her daughter Mary, who was to become his biographer. In a letter to Mrs Besant, Lady Emily gave a vivid picture of him at this time:

It is very curious to watch the phases through which Krishna passes. Sometimes he is just a frolicsome boy with apparently not a serious thought in the world. Then swiftly he changes and becomes the Teacher stern and uncompromising, urging his pupils onward towards swift progress. Again he is just tortured with the pain in his spine, not speaking and just wanting quiet, or most strange of all the figure that comes to dinner, beautiful, with unseeing eyes, mechanically eating his food and shrinking at every sound. Most beautiful of all is when he sits in meditation chanting mantrams, his soul going out in worship. These phases succeed each other in such swift succession that it is something of a strain to be always prepared for them.[32]

The pain in his spine could be understood as caused by the awakening of the *kundalini* force, although Leadbeater who believed that his own *kundalini* had been awakened some years before, was at a loss to understand all the other symptoms that Krishnamurti manifested: his behaving like one possessed, moaning, groaning and muttering incoherently; his extreme sensitivity to sound and revulsion to the touch of anyone; his loss of control of his body and tendency to fall over. It could be considered that the extreme form of 'the process' was commensurate with Krishnamurti's unique destined role in the world. Nitya even wrote to Leadbeater asking: 'Do you know at all if something similar to what is going on now was part of the preparation of Master Jesus when the Lord came last time?' In reply, Leadbeater confessed: 'I don't understand the terrible drama that is taking place with our beloved Krishna.'[32] Nitya's interpretation, however, appeared to be supported by a message that Krishnamurti himself 'brought through' ostensibly from 'the Masters', one night in November 1923. The message went:

> The work that is being done now is of gravest importance and exceedingly delicate. It is the first time that this experiment is being carried out in the world. Everything in the household must give way to this work, and no one's convenience must be considered, not even Krishna's. Strangers must not come there too often, the strain is too great. You and Krishna can work this out.[32]

'The process' culminated, in February 1924, in an experience which Krishnamurti described in the following words:

I had an extraordinary evening. Whatever it is, the force or whatever one calls the bally thing, came up my spine, up to the nape of my neck, then it separated into two, one going to the right and the other to the left of my head till they met between the two eyes, just above my nose. There was a kind of flame and I saw the Lord and Master. It was a tremendous night.[32]

The yogic explanation of the experience that Krishnamurti thus described would be, of course, that it was the opening of the 'third eye', or '*Ajna chakra*', in the middle of the brow, which signifies the heightening of self-awareness and the expansion of mental powers, and the way that Krishnamurti's teaching developed after he had gone through 'the process' could certainly be cited as evidence to support such an explanation.

3

The Coming Gone Wrong

As head of the Order of the Star in the East (OSE), Krishnamurti became, in the 1920s, a man of property. In 1921 Baron Philip van Pallandt offered him, as a personal gift, his Castle Eerde at Ommen in Holland, together with an estate of 5000 acres of land. Krishnamurti accepted it on behalf of the Order, of which it became the headquarters. Then, in 1923, an American benefactress bought the cottage at Ojai for them, together with thirteen acres of land. In 1925, on a visit to his birthplace, Madanapalle in southern India, Krishnamurti conceived the idea of establishing a university there, and the following year he was able to buy 300 acres of land in lovely country near the town, where a school was founded. With these and other properties, with first-class world-wide travel provided for him and wealthy patrons to be found wherever he appeared, not to mention a private income of £500 settled upon him by the American benefactress, Miss Dodge, the head of the OSE had an enviable life. That many people should have been incredulous, and others aggrieved, when he later renounced his office and disbanded the Order, is hardly surprising.

A severe blow to Krishnamurti's own belief in the OSE's purpose, and in the wisdom, power and benevolence of the Masters, must have been administered by the death of Nitya in November 1925. Krishnamurti was on his way to India with Mrs Besant at the time. When, on the morning of the 14th, she broke the news to him that Nitya had died in Ojai a few hours before, he was shattered, and so was his philosophy of life – the Theosophical view according to which Nitya had a vital function to perform in the ministry of the World Teacher. Only the day before, when he had received a telegram from Nitya saying that his illness had become more serious, Krishnamurti had told a friend: 'If Nitya was to die I would not have been allowed to leave Ojai.' This statement demonstrated a degree of confidence and belief in the Masters which must have been severely shaken by his brother's death.

A tenet of the later Krishnamurti teaching is that we should stay with our pains and sufferings, and should not employ thought and ideas as means of escaping from, or alleviating, them. According to his friend Shiva Rao, who shared a cabin with him during the voyage, Krishnamurti stayed with his grief for ten days, during which time he was inconsolable, sobbing, moaning and hardly speaking to anyone, but then he appears to have emerged with a kind of intellectual reconciliation to Nitya's death, for he wrote:

The pleasant dreams my brother and I had of the physical are over. . . An old dream is dead and a new one is being born, as a flower that pushes through the solid earth. . . On the physical plane we could be separated and now we are inseparable. For my brother and I are one. As Krishnamurti I now have greater zeal, greater faith, greater sympathy and greater love for there is also in me the body, the Being, of Nityananda.[32]

The purpose of the trip to India was to attend the Theosophical Society Convention, which was held at Adyar from 24 to 27 December 1925. The following day, the 28th, was the fourteenth anniversary of the famous 'visitation' of the Lord Maitreya to the young Krishnamurti, and on the sacred day an OSE Congress was held. On this occasion there occurred an event even stranger than the 'visitation'. Krishnamurti gave a talk to the assembly on the subject of the World Teacher, and suddenly towards the end of it, in the middle of a sentence, the timbre of his voice changed and he began to speak in the first person. 'He comes not only to those who want, who desire, who long,' he said, then went on: 'and I come for those who want sympathy, who want happiness, who are longing to be released, who are longing to find happiness in all things. I come to reform and not to tear down, I come not to destroy but to build.'[32]

Mrs Besant was in no doubt as to what this dramatic change in Krishnamurti's delivery meant. 'The coming has begun,' she told the Congress, and said that the event signified 'the final acceptance of the body chosen long before.' Krishnamurti himself seems to have believed in the Theosophical interpretation and, without any sense of personal pride, to have believed that he was serving as the vehicle for the Lord Maitreya. 'I personally feel quite different from that day,' he said, and compared himself to a vessel which had been so purified that 'anyone in the world can put a beautiful flower in it and the flower shall live in the vase and never die.'[32] He was sure, he said, that the Lord would come again soon, and that it would be 'a nobler and far more beautiful occasion than even last time.'

The occasion when everyone expected another manifestation of the Lord through his chosen vehicle was at the next OSE Convention, which was held in July 1926 at Castle Eerde, and was attended by some 2000 people. Their expectations were not disappointed. Again, towards the end of his address, Krishnamurti broke into phrases of scriptural resonance couched in the first person. In the published version of his talks, they are even set out in blank verse:

> I belong to all people, to all who really love, to all who are suffering.
> And if you would walk, you must walk with me.
> And if you would understand, you must look through my mind.
> And if you would feel, you must look through my heart.
> And because I really love, I want you to love.
> Because I really feel, I want you to feel.
> Because I hold everything dear, I want you to hold all things dear.
> Because I want to protect, you should protect.
> And this is the only life worth living, and the only
> Happiness worth possessing.[1]

The question whether Krishnamurti was literally inspired to make such pronouncements, and whether he uttered them spontaneously, as he presumably would if they were the words of the Lord Maitreya, is a bit of a puzzle, particularly as they are printed in a volume entitled *Early Writings*. One cannot but wonder whether there was not, perhaps at a subconscious level, an element of role-playing and even self-deception in the way that Krishnamurti was speaking at this time, which would explain the vehemence of his reaction three years later. In 1929 he spurned his followers, but in his 1926 Ommen talk he had said:

> I would make all of you drink at my fountain, I would make all of you breathe that scented air, so that you can yourselves become creators, geniuses, who make the world happy... For this reason you must awaken, you must walk along with me and follow.[1]

This was the sort of thing that Theosophists expected of the World Teacher, and however little sympathy one may have for the mentality of the blind follower, Krishnamurti's later repudiation of the response that he had so eloquently elicited does seem a little harsh.

At this time he was also advocating principles to which his later teachings were diametrically opposed. He was, for instance, urging people to strive, to be ambitious in their aspirations towards the spiritual life, to pursue growth through disciplined efforts of the mind and will. 'Use your mind to drive you to your particular goal,' he urged the people at Ommen, and he told them 'it is important that you should understand with your mind.'[1] But two of the recurrent and central themes in his later teaching are that the operations of the mind, of thought, serve only to confuse and obscure our perception of reality, and that deliberately to pursue the goal of spiritual development is a self-defeating enterprise, for its sets up conflicts which consume the energy needed for the very process of development.

That there should be discrepancies and turn-abouts in a man's thinking over the course of a lifetime is not a thing to be wondered at, but it does rather derogate from any claim to be privy to revealed truth or to speak with the authority of a Master (although Krishnamurti himself never made such claims, they were implicit in the role the Theosophists assigned him). Most of Krishnamurti's utterances during the years 1926–27 tended towards the mystical and rapturous, and contrast conspicuously with his later, lucid, spare, no-nonsense manner. He spoke frequently of experiencing union with 'the Beloved': an experience which clearly meant a great deal to him, though he was teasingly inexplicit as to what it meant for his followers.

'What you are troubling about,' he told them, 'is whether there is such a person as the World Teacher who has manifested himself in the body of a certain person, Krishnamurti; but in the world nobody will trouble about this question. So you will see my point of view when I speak of my Beloved. It is an unfortunate thing that I have to explain, but I must. I want it to be as vague as possible, and I hope I have made it so. My Beloved is the open skies, the flower, every human being. . . . Till I was able to say with certainty, without any undue excitement, or exaggeration in order to convince others, that I was one with my Beloved. . .I talked of vague generalities which everyone wanted. I never said: I am the World Teacher: but now that I feel that I am one with the Beloved, I say it, not in order to impress my authority on you, not to convince you of my greatness, nor of the greatness of the World Teacher, nor even of the beauty of life, the simplicity of life, but merely to awaken the desire in your hearts and in your minds to seek out the Truth.[1]

If he was somewhat ambiguous with his public, he was not so with his close associates. He wrote to Mrs Besant: 'More and more I am certain that I am the Teacher and my mind and consciousness is changed.' And to Leadbeater:

> I know my destiny and my work. I know with certainty and knowledge of my own that I am blending into the consciousness of the one Teacher and that He will completely fill me up. I feel and I know that my cup is nearly full to the brim and that it will overflow soon. Till then I must abide quietly, and with eager patience... I long to make, and I will make, everybody happy.[32]

To make everybody happy is by no means a discreditable aim for a World Teacher, but it is quite a different matter from the purpose that Krishnamurti was proclaiming two years later: 'to set man free'. These years saw the great transition of Krishnamurti's life: from the mystic to the emancipator; from the gentle teacher with eloquent and extravagant turns of phrase to the stern moralist and trenchant castigator of all modes of human escapism, idleness, inauthenticity and self-deception; from the public figure, revered by some and derided by many for being proclaimed the Christ become incarnate again, to the very private figure, the simple, solitary man without any attachments or pretensions.

What brought about the change? In one of his most revealing autobiographical passages, he explained:

> Like everyone else, Krishnamurti, in the past, searched, obeyed and worshipped, but as time grew, as suffering came, he wanted to discover the reality which hides behind the picture, behind the sunset, behind the image, behind all philosophies, behind all religions, all sects, all organisations; and to discover and to understand that, he had to hang on to a peg of unreality, of untruth, till, little by little, he was able to pass all those shrines that are limiting, that are binding, all the gods that insist on worship. In passing all those he was able to arrive where all religions, where all affections are consummated, where all worship ends, where all desire ceases, where the separate self is purified by being destroyed. It is because I have gone through those stages that I am able to speak with the authority of my own experience, with the authority of my own knowledge, and I would give to you of that knowledge, of that experience.[1]

Having arrived 'where worship ends' and having learnt to speak with the authority of his own experience and his own knowledge, Krishnamurti naturally felt himself in a false position as a figure whom people worshipped and looked up to for guidance and understanding. Even Mrs Besant had declared herself his disciple, and when she was present at his speeches she no longer sat beside him on the dais, but sat on the ground at his feet. In 1927 and 1928 Krishnamurti's talks at the OSE and Theosophical Society meeting showed increasing impatience with such attitudes, and irritation at the way that he was bound and limited by the image that people had of him. 'Because you have been accustomed for centuries to labels, you want life to be labelled,' he told OSE members. 'You want Krishnamurti to be labelled, and in a definite manner, so that you can say: Now I understand – and then you think there will be peace within you. I am afraid it is not going to be that way.'[1]

He foresaw that if his followers had their way a new religion would be built up around him. 'You will build a temple,' he predicted,

> you will set about forming rules in your minds, because the individual, Krishnamurti has represented to you the Truth. So you will build a temple, you will then begin to have ceremonies, to invent phrases, dogmas, systems of beliefs, creeds, and to create philosophies. If you build great foundations upon me, the individual, you will be caught in that house, that temple, and you will have to have another Teacher come and extricate you from that temple, pull you out of the narrowness in order to liberate you.[1]

Sometimes he became severe almost to the point of insult in his efforts to disembarrass himself of his following. 'How happy you would be if I decided for you,' he told one gathering. 'You are all like little children who cannot stand on their own feet and walk by themselves. You have been preparing for seventeen years, and you are caught in your own creation.' And what, he asked, would the people of the world at large care for the teachings of Theosophy, and what would they care about the question of his own role and identity which his followers set such importance on?

> The people of the world are not concerned with whether it is a manifestation, or an indwelling, or a visitation into the tabernacle prepared for many years, or Krishnamurti himself. What they are going to say is: I am suffering, I have my passing pleasures and changing sorrows. Have you anything lasting to give?[1]

Krishnamurti believed that he had something lasting to give. He had his own experience and his own understanding of life; he had, above all, the knowledge with which to set man free – free as he had become 'from all cages, from all fears... religions... sects... theories... philosophies', free through the exercise of awareness for the only thing worthwhile: the apprehension of Truth. Of course, he could not convey it within the confines of the belief system of Theosophy and the OSE. As he now saw it, liberation from all belief systems was the prerequisite of true freedom, so the next step he had to take was the formal dissolution of the movement that had been building around him for nearly two decades. It was a step that required an extraordinary resolution and courage: the courage to be a disappointment to thousands of people, to deny them the comfort and consolation that they had found in their beliefs, and to make them take a straight, undistorted look at the thing that for the most part they were least able or disposed to look at honestly – themselves.

Krishnamurti formally dissolved the Order of the Star at the Ommen Convention in 1929, on 3 August, with a speech delivered to a gathering of 3000 people. Explaining the reasons for his decision, he said:

> I maintain that Truth is a pathless land, and you cannot approach it by any path whatsoever, by any religion, by any sect... Truth cannot be organized; nor should any organization be formed to lead or coerce people along any particular path... Truth cannot be brought down, rather the individual must make the effort to ascend to it.[32]

Referring to his renouncing his position as head of the Order, he went on:

> This is no magnificent deed, because I do not want followers, and I mean this. The moment you follow someone you cease to follow Truth. I am not concerned whether you pay attention to what I say or not. I want to do a certain thing in the world and I am going to do it with an unwavering concentration. I am concerning myself with only one essential thing: to set man free... If there are only five people who will listen, who will live, who have their faces turned towards eternity, it will be sufficient... Because I am free, unconditioned, whole, not the part, not the relative, but the whole Truth that is eternal, I desire those who seek to understand me, to be free, not to follow me, not to make out of me a cage which will become a religion, a sect.[32]

He urged his listeners to take a look at themselves, to consider whether any real and fundamental change had taken place in them as a consequence of their being members of the OSE and having heard his talks over the years. 'You are all depending for your spirituality on someone else, for your happiness on someone else, for your enlightenment on someone else,' he told them, and

> when I say look within yourselves for the enlightenment, for the glory, for the purification and for the incorruptibility of the self, not one of you is willing to do it. There may be a few, but very, very few. So why have an organization? ... Those who really desire to understand, who are looking to find that which is eternal, without a beginning and without an end, will walk together with greater intensity, will be a danger to everything that is unessential, to unrealities, to shadows ... And they will concentrate, they will become the flame, because they understand. Such a body we must create, and this is my purpose.[32]

Mrs Besant and the leading Theosophists had often said that the teachings of the World Teacher, when he came among them, would probably be quite different from anything they had preconceived and hoped for, and that people should remain open to the new and the unexpected, but what Krishnamurti was now saying was so unexpected, so incompatible with the teachings and prophesies of Theosophy, that they were unable to heed their own warnings and advice. Mrs Besant herself never made publicly known the disappointment and disillusionment that she felt, but Leadbeater expressed the feelings of many when he delivered himself of the preposterous statement that 'the Coming has gone wrong'.

4
Exploring the Pathless Land

LIBERATING himself from the incumbency of his position as head of the OSE and his public image as Messiah-figure no doubt gave Krishnamurti great personal satisfaction and relief, but outwardly his life did not change very much. The properties of the Order were returned to their donors, but Krishnamurti continued to speak regularly to gatherings of people at Ommen, at Ojai and in India, although now these meetings were open to the general public. He was also invited to speak in many other countries, to widely varying assemblies of people. Invariably he accepted, spurred on by his desire to convey his experience of the joy of the totally liberated life and to encourage others to discover it in and for themselves.

In relation to his audiences, Krishnamurti gradually developed a unique manner and approach. This was consistent with his refusal to be an authority and with his purpose of seeking out the few who would really listen to him and be helped by his experience to become liberated and creative themselves. 'Don't agree or disagree with what I say,' he would tell his audiences. 'Let us go into this together ... let us inquire ... look into it more deeply ... go slowly ... really look at it.' He was impatient with glib questions and premature conclusions, but always extremely courteous with the members of his audience, addressing each one as 'Sir', not out of deference but in order, by reversing the conventional speaker-questioner protocol, to keep them mindful of the fact that they were not there just to listen respectfully to the speaker but to participate in a dialogue and an inquiry.

Krishnamurti's own investigations of the many aspects of the truth that he had discovered went on for many years; different aspects of it were given prominence at different times as the circumstances of life – both of his own life and of life in the world at large – determined. His talks and writings of the 1930s and later were not simply expository, however, but were part of a lifelong engagement in the task of rendering as clearly and precisely as possible the results of his experience and his investigations. This was no easy task, for 'truth is a pathless land', and language (like organizations) has a tendency to constrain and distort it. The experience central to Krishnamurti's developing philosophy of life was what he variously referred to as 'the death of the self', 'the disappearance of the "I"', or the annihilation of individuality achieved through union with life itself. The language capable of getting his meaning across eluded him; even people eager to understand were perplexed by his attempts to express it. Sometimes they suspected that his valuing and cultivating an experience of such an ineffable nature was a kind of escapism.

To one person who expressed such thoughts, his friend Lady Emily Lutyens, whose failure to understand distressed him, he wrote an explanation and protest which gives an illuminating insight into the man:

> I am sorry that you feel that way about what I say. The ecstasy that I feel is the outcome of this world. I wanted to understand, I wanted to conquer sorrow, this pain of detachment and attachment, death, continuity of life, everything that man goes through, every day. I wanted to understand and conquer it. I have. So my ecstasy is real and infinite, not an escape. I know the way out of this incessant misery and I want to help people out of the bog of this sorrow. No, this is not an escape.[32]

We shall consider the stages through which Krishnamurti went and the ideas he formulated in attempting to convey his fundamental perception and experience of life later in the book. But, in passing, we may note that one development that helped elucidate his thought in the early 1930s were his ruminations on the nature of time and memory. It is fascinating to note that his biographer says that at about this time he lost his memory of the past almost completely. This, she suggests, 'was consistent with his teaching that memory, except for practical purposes, was a dead-weight that should not be carried over from one day to another; death to each day was constant rebirth.'[32] Yes, indeed, but for a philosopher to carry consistency between his thought and his life to such lengths is surely remarkable.

Mary Lutyens also tells us that in the course of his development Krishnamurti manifested psychic powers, particularly clairvoyance and the ability to effect healings. But he rarely exercised them: he regarded clairvoyance as an intrusion of privacy, and did not wish to become known as a healer because he did not want people to come to him just for physical healing.

The 1930s and 40s were decades when, as Thomas Mann put it, 'the destiny of man expressed itself in political terms'. Total war, senseless violence, ideological tub-thumping, and political and economic catastrophes testified to the fact that human beings were pitifully deficient in the ability to foresee and control the consequences of their fears, greeds, envies and stupidities when they were projected and magnified on the world stage. Political events dramatically demonstrated the disastrous results of things that Krishnamurti had attacked in the context of the OSE: the follow-my-leader mentality, and the tendency of the human mind to seek a path out of its confusion by way of belief in an ideology.

Krishnamurti now extended his diagnosis of the ills of man and society to the world at large, becoming the tireless advocate of what he considered the only revolution that could be effective in the circumstances – a transformation of human nature, an evolutionary great leap forward. Such advocacy was, of course, impugned as idealistic and unrealistic. But Krishnamurti knew from experience that individual human nature could be completely transformed. As all the world's troubles were obviously the projection of the failings of unregenerate man, it followed that their solution could only be accomplished through such a transformation. What was truly unrealistic was to expect change to be effected by administering more of the same medicine – more organization, systematization and subordination of the aspirations of the individual to some myth of the ultimate collective good – for that had already been seen to aggravate rather than cure the ills of man and society.

So Krishnamurti became identified in the minds of many with political anarchists, and he came under attack for having a negative attitude at a time that called for positive action. He replied to this charge:

> You who are always shouting at me for my negative attitude, what are you doing now to wipe out the very cause of war itself? I am talking about the real cause of all wars, not only of the immediate war that inevitably threatens while each nation is piling up armaments. As long as the spirit of nationalism exists, the spirit of class distinctions, of

particularity and possessiveness, there must be war. If you are really facing the problem of war, as you should be now, you will have to take a definite action, a definite, positive action: and by your action you will help to awaken intelligence, which is the only preventive of war. But to do that you must free yourself of the disease of 'my God, my country, my family, my house'.[35]

Throughout the 1930s, Krishnamurti had travelled widely, in Europe, India and the United States, giving talks, often to audiences of thousands. His life and travels were financed partly by benefactors and partly by the sale of publications issued by the Star Publishing Trust, which had been set up for the purpose, and published not only his early writings but also the monthly *Star Review*. With the coming of the Second World War all this activity was perforce halted, and he spent the duration at Ojai in California. There were friends and associates with and near him, and he had many visitors who often travelled far to see him, but the war years were a relatively inactive time for him. He discovered new occupations, such as cultivating vegetables, and keeping chickens, cows and bees. He also spent more time writing, and took long daily walks in the mountains. Walking was, and remained throughout his life, a mode of meditation for Krishnamurti, though this was clearly not understood at the time by the FBI, who sent an agent to ask him why he walked so much and whom he met, apparently because they suspected him of being involved in a plot to assassinate President Roosevelt. It was as well he didn't speak in public during the war, for he certainly would not have mitigated his pacifist and anti-partisan views and the FBI would not have taken kindly to such statements as: 'War is a spectacular expression of the brutalities, exploitations and narrowness of our daily conduct.' He would have been packed off to India as an undesirable alien in no time. So, instead, he cultivated his garden and talked only to friends.

One of those friends was the writer Aldous Huxley: Huxley, the man who reputedly read encyclopaedias from cover to cover, the polymath intellectual, the man of knowledge, the seeming very antithesis of Krishnamurti. It was a strange relationship, as Krishnamurti himself said later (writing of himself, as he always did, in the third person):

> To go for a walk with him was a delight. He would discourse on the wayside flowers and, though he couldn't see properly, whenever we passed in the hills of California an animal close by, he would name it,

and develop the destructive nature of modern civilisation and its violence. Krishnamurti would help him to cross a stream or a pothole. These two had a strange relationship with each other, affectionate, considerate and it seems non-verbal communication. They would often be sitting together without saying a word.[33]

Huxley urged Krishnamurti to write; in response Krishnamurti produced a number of short pieces based upon his experiences and meetings with people, each comprising introductory paragraphs of description of a place or person followed by a dialogue. Enthusing about the originality of the first pieces he was shown, Huxley encouraged Krishnamurti to continue, and the result was the first volume of the *Commentaries on Living* series. At this time, Huxley was a writer of world renown, and the part he played in getting Krishnamurti known to a wider audience cannot be underestimated. He wrote a long Introduction to *The First and Last Freedom* (1954), Krishnamurti's first substantial statement of his philosophy to be issued by major publishing houses in Britain and the United States, which no doubt contributed to the book's immense success.

Although many books appeared under Krishnamurti's name after this, most of them were transcripts of his talks and discussions. Those he actually wrote have a particular interest as revelations of the quality of his mind and awareness, and I propose to discuss these later. He was tireless in his work of – as he put it – 'going around the world trying to point out truth', and in setting up schools, which were the only institutions that he would allow to be associated with his name, and writing was something that he did intermittently. In 1946 the Happy Valley School was opened near Ojai, with Huxley as one of the trustees. Schools in India, the first at Rishi Valley near his birthplace, Madanapalle, and the second at Rajghat, near Benares, had been opened in 1928 and 1934. When the Second World War was over Krishnamurti was eager to return to India to visit them. However, his departure was delayed by a severe illness, a kidney infection which laid him low for months, and it was not until late in 1947 that he was able to make the journey.

India as an independent nation was only a few months old and was in the throes of violent political and sectarian upheaval, with Hindus and Muslims slaughtering each other. Jawaharlal Nehru was Prime Minister, and Mahatma Gandhi, whose shrewd strategies of non-violent resistance had precipitated the ending of British colonial rule, was the nation's spiritual *éminence grise*. A few weeks after Krishnamurti's arrival, India and the world were stunned by the news of Gandhi's assassination. Two days after the event, Krishnamurti was asked at a public meeting to comment on it, and his response, characteristically, was uncompromising and put the questioner on the spot:

> I wonder what your reaction was when you heard the news. What was your response? Were you concerned over it as a personal loss, or as an indication of the trend of world events? World events are not unrelated incidents; they are related. The real cause of Gandhiji's untimely death lies in you. The real cause is you. Because you are communal, you encourage the spirit of division – through property, through caste, through ideology, through having different religions, sects, leaders. When you call yourself a Hindu, a Muslim, a Parsee, or God knows what else, it is bound to produce conflict in the world.[31]

Krishnamurti always insisted that he had no nationality; although he acknowledged his origins he denied that he was an Indian. Yet in India he was always held in the high esteem that culture and tradition accord the holy man or religious teacher, not only by the lowly multitudes who turned out to hear him speak, but also by the learned and powerful. He was, despite his disclaimers, long absence and political non-partisanship, a renowned and respected figure in India. He had met both Gandhi and Nehru in the 1930s, arguing with the latter that throughout history India had stood for the religious spirit and unless that were first regenerated the political struggle would accomplish nothing. Nehru had argued that political freedom must come first, to give the spirit space to develop. Now the two men met again, at the Prime Minister's request, not long after Gandhi's murder. Nehru was no longer the ardent young nationalist, but a man burdened with the responsibilities of office, deeply distressed by the uncontrollable eruptions of sectarian violence that were threatening to disintegrate the new nation. Pupul Jayakar, a close friend of Krishnamurti's who was later to become one of his biographers, was present at the meeting. From her recollection of the gist of the long conversation, we receive the impression that Nehru was no longer a man arguing a point of view but rather one seeking spiritual sustenance in his personal anguish. They talked about the contest between the forces of good and evil in the world, about the nature of right action and right thought, about the relationship between individual and social transformation, and how disorder and division in society are a projection of the same characteristics in individuals. If the discussion did not help Nehru the politician very much, it clearly meant a great deal to Nehru the man, for the two parted affectionately and arranged to meet again, which they did a few months later.

After the enforced relative inactivity of the war years and his long sojourn at Ojai, Krishnamurti threw himself into his work in India with great vigour. Public talks to large audiences, the affairs of the schools, meetings with individuals who sought his help or to work with him, discussions with scholars, politicians, friends and associates, old and new, kept him intensely busy. After eight months he was persuaded to take a rest at a house in the hill station of Ootacamund ('Ooty.'), near Madras. Pupul Jayakar and her sister Nandini Mehta were staying nearby, and over a period of three weeks they witnessed what appears from their record to have been a repetition of the experience that Krishnamurti had undergone at Ojai in 1922.

The sisters accompanied him on his daily walks, and one evening he asked them to return to the house with him. He seemed to be in great pain and they proposed getting a doctor, which he forbade them to do, asking them just to sit with him and look after 'the body', closing his mouth if he fainted. The pain came in spasms, intensifying in the nape of the neck, the spine, the crown of the head and the stomach, accompanied by fits of shivering, and sometimes by Krishnamurti speaking, in a frail, childlike voice, talking about his long-dead brother Nitya or calling out for Krishnamurti to return to the body, which to the observers was just a shell lying and tossing on the bed. The episode lasted for about two hours, and towards the end of it the voice said Krishnamurti was coming back and spoke of his being accompanied by others, who were 'spotless, untouched, pure'. Then the frail body changed, 'filled with a soaring presence' which seemed to envelope the entire room, and Krishnamurti was back.

There were a series of episodes like this over the three weeks. always occurring in the evening. Sometimes the sisters would accompany him on a walk, sometimes he wanted to go alone, but on other occasions he was already too weak and in too much pain to go out. The pain seemed excruciating, it contorted his face and body, made him weep and sweat. He said he couldn't stop it, any more than a woman in labour could stop having a child. Once when it was beginning he said, 'They are going to have fun with me tonight. I see the storm gathering.' Other statements he made that showed an awareness of what was happening were: 'They are cleansing the brain, oh, so completely, emptying it', 'They have burnt me so that there can be more emptiness. They want to see how much of him can come through', and 'I know what they are up to ... They know how much the body can stand ... They are very careful with the body.' States of semi-consciousness when he could speak through the pain and about it would give way to periods of unconsciousness when the body seemed just a tortured or inert object. If he spoke then it was in the childlike voice, and references to himself were in the third person. Once he spoke of something having happened when he was out on his walk and he asked if they had seen him return. 'They came and covered him with leaves,' he said, and 'Do you know, you would not have seen him tomorrow. He nearly did not return.' Then he started to come to, and felt his body as if to see if it were all there, saying 'I don't know whether I returned. There may be pieces of me in the road.'[31]

Despite his apparent awareness of what was happening and his assurance that 'they' knew what they were doing and would protect the body, he seemed also to be aware that during these episodes he came very close to death. Once he asked Nandini to hold his hand, lest he should slip away and not come back. But when he did come back he showed no after-effects of what he had been through. 'He was aflame with energy – joyous, eager, and youthful,' writes Pupul Jayakar. What most impressed the sisters was the manner of his returning; the way the body filled out, seemed to grow, and to be imbued with tremendous power, and the room filled with a throbbing energy. These effects were most pronounced at the end of what turned out to be the final episode. Then Krishnamurti asked the sisters, 'Did you see that face?' and told them, 'The Buddha was here. You are blessed.'[31]

Krishnamurti did not subsequently write or talk about these experiences, as he had done about the 1922 Ojai experiences. Then he had waxed lyrical and ecstatic about what had happened to him, but now, twenty-six years on, having put behind him the language and expectations of Theosophy and developed the view that memory and interpretation only distort experiences, he was more reticent. Not until years later did he mention the experiences to the sisters again, and then only briefly in letters he wrote to them from London, where apparently he was undergoing yet another onset of 'the process'. In these letters, written in May 1961, he referred to 'the wheels of Ooty', saying they were working 'powerfully', 'furiously', 'painfully'. It was the only clue he gave to his understanding of 'the process': his use of the term 'wheels', clearly, referring to the *chakras*, which are commonly represented as wheels illustrations of Indian occult anatomy.

When he arrived in India, on this and later occasions, Krishnamurti always discarded his Western clothes and adopted Indian ones, which made his rejection of the role of guru the more difficult because he looked the part. Indians found it hard to comprehend that a religious teacher should decline to dispense blessings or to have a following and an entourage of disciples, and that he should discourage expressions of reverence and devotion that were the holy man's due. Whenever he saw someone about to bow to him, he would pre-empt the obeisance by touching the feet of the devotee, and although he could not always prevent people touching him or his robes he did not conceal the fact that he found the gestures inappropriate and embarrassing. India, as he had said to Nehru, had throughout history represented the religious spirit, but the survival of that tradition in rituals and practices divested of true spirituality was a hindrance rather than a help to the communication of the teachings. Scholars who were wont to dwell on correspondences between the teachings and the philosophy of Vedanta and the Upanishads were as far from grasping their import as were the multitudes (sometimes three or four thousand) who congregated to listen to his talks, believing that merely being in the presence of an acknowledged great religious teacher conferred a spiritual benefit. Religiosity, whether of the scholarly or superstitious variety, was to Krishnamurti a kind of spiritual inertia to which the Indian mind was particularly prone, and he was vehement in castigating it. 'People use the guru as a crutch,' he told someone who asked him why he rejected the role. Of the sannyasis, the revered mendicant monks of India whose saffron robes betoken a renunciation of all things worldly, he said that their austerities, devotions, meditations and immersion in the scriptures did not constitute the religious life. 'Putting on a saffron robe does not mean renouncing,' he said. 'You can never renounce the world, because the world is part of you. You renounce a few cows, a house, but to renounce your heredity, your tradition, the burden of your condition, that demands enormous enquiry.'[31]

There was an ambivalence, though, in Krishnamurti's feelings about India and its culture. His vehemence was proportionate to his affection for a land and people that, for all his denial of nationality in principle, in spirit were his familiars and kin. Critical though he was of the sannyasis in general, he always made himself available and had a warm welcome for individuals who came to see him. For the Buddha he always had a particular affection. One of his favourite walks was along the pilgrim's path to Sarnath, the place of the Buddha's Enlightenment, which runs through the grounds of the school at Rajghat. He knew some Sanskrit, and was sometimes heard chanting verses in the language. He began each day with a routine of *asanas*, or yoga exercises, though he stressed that the practice was in no way religious or ritualistic. He chose to have an Indian passport, when he could have opted for a British one. Wherever he went in the world he inveighed against sectarianism and nationalism, the corruption of spirit and intelligence by politics, and the misdirection of the religious aspirations into creeds, dogmas and rituals. In India his denunciations were sterner and more incisive than elsewhere, no doubt partly because these faults were the more exaggerated in the aftermath of Independence, but also, one feels, because he had a special love of the land and people of India and a native understanding of their potentials as well as their failings.

5

'The Flowering'

THE 1950s and 60s were years of consolidation: of the teachings in Krishnamurti's published books, of his reputation with a general and world-wide public through the books, and of the nucleus of associates who helped organize his schedules of talks and extend the network of schools. His work of 'going around the world trying to point out truth' took him to New York, London, Paris, Rome, Amsterdam, Brussels, Athens, Colombo, Sydney and numerous other places, as well as his home bases in India and California. Among his close friends in Europe were the Scavarellis, Vanda and Luigi, an aristocratic and artistic Florentine couple. It was through them that, in 1961, he started holding annual gatherings at Saanen near Gstaad in Switzerland, which continued until the year before his death. The Swiss landscape became, like those of India and Ojai, especially dear to him, inspiring some of his finest descriptive writing about nature. Several of the series of talks that he gave at Saanen, which were later published as books, are among the most powerful and eloquent statements of his philosophy.

Although Krishnamurti put tremendous energy into everything he did, his talks, his walks, his travels, he was not robust, and, although his dietary and exercise regimes were exemplary, he was frequently laid low by illness. Bronchitis and hay fever troubled him throughout his life, as did proneness to faints, fevers and kidney infections. In his later years he had prostate and hernia operations, as well as suffering from diabetes and the pancreatic cancer that eventually killed him. Often when he was ill he told those looking after him that he felt he could easily 'slip away', and that only the thought of what he had yet to do gave him the strength to shut death's door when it would have been much easier to pass through it. He did, apparently, temporarily 'go off' during his illnesses, just as he did during onsets of 'the process'. At Ooty he had stressed to the sisters that they must on no account call a doctor: clearly he knew how to tell between the two kinds of affliction, but the distinction was not always obvious to others. Once when he was ill with a fever in Rome he began to talk about himself in the third person again and Vanda Scavarelli wrote down what he said:

> He has gone far away, very far away. It has been told to you to look after him ... Nice face to look at. Those eyelashes are wasted for a man. Why don't you take them? That face has been carefully worked out. They have worked and worked for so long, so many centuries, to produce such a body. Do you know him? You cannot know him. How can you know the running water? ... The body has been all this time on the edge of a precipice. It has been held, it has been watched like mad all these months, and if he lets go he will go very far. Death is very near...[33]

Such statements may be put down to feverish delirium, but that doesn't necessarily discredit them as insights into Krishnamurti's mind and expressions of his awareness of what he was. Some might regard them as revealing a loss of hold upon reality, but they could on the other hand be flashes of insight into reality. Certainly the proximity of death in life is a reality that most of us shun, and one wonders whether it would have figured so prominently as a theme in the teachings or been so forcefully expounded there but for Krishnamurti's personal experiences of illness.

Krishnamurti had close ties with England. It was the home of many of his closest and oldest friends – the country where he had spent much of his youth and had been educated. His primary language was English, as was the literature he loved best. In his youthful writings he was influenced by Shakespeare and the Romantic poets, especially Keats. His style in dress, manners and speech, was essentially, sometimes idiosyncratically, English. ('By Jove' was a favourite exclamation.) Over the years he paid regular visits to London, sometimes staying for several weeks to give a series of talks. But it was not until 1968 that the English Krishnamurti Foundation was able to afford a permanent base and establish a school. This was at Brockwood Park in Hampshire, a large Georgian country house set in its own park land. From then on Krishnamurti spent two or three months at Brockwood each year, giving a series of talks in August which attracted large gatherings, mostly of young people who would camp in the grounds. The school flourished and after a few years had a full complement of sixty pupils.

The late 1960s and the 70s saw the emergence in the West of a 'counter culture' which rejected the values and lifestyle of the established culture, particularly its materialism, conformism, utilitarianism and consumerism, espousing an alternative world-view and lifestyle which gave priority to spirituality, spontaneity, nonconformism and 'voluntary simplicity'. Many young people were attracted to Eastern religions and to guru-figures, such as the Maharishi Mahesh Yogi and Sri Rajneesh, who had no reservations about adopting the Indian holy-man role and mystique, actively seeking and encouraging a following. They skilfully exploited the media and high-profile media figures for this purpose, and comported themselves with conspicuous flamboyance and authority. All this, of course, was anathema to Krishnamurti, who knew from experience how easy and ultimately pointless it was to exploit people's spiritual malaise and aspirations. He would have nothing to do with what he sometimes referred to as the popular gurus' travelling circus. Pupul Jayakar has an amusing anecdote about a meeting between Krishnamurti and the Maharishi. They happened to be on the same flight from Europe to India. Soon after departure a hostess presented Krishnamurti with a rose, saying that the Maharishi sent it with his greetings. He accepted the gift and asked her to thank the Maharishi. Some time later, returning from the toilet, he passed the bearded guru, sitting cross-legged on a tiger skin, and was pressed to sit beside him for a while and talk. The Maharishi talked about his work in Nepal, where he said he was going to initiate a world revolution in consciousness. He urged Krishnamurti to join him in the work, because he believed that together they could change humanity. With characteristic courtesy, Krishnamurti declined the invitation, saying that at present he had a number of rather pressing engagements. The Maharishi, one must assume, understood neither Krishnamurti's sly sense of humour nor the fundamentals of his teaching, for he continued for some time to urge the liaison. Krishnamurti eventually returned to his seat for the rest of the journey, and when they arrived at New Delhi he passed unnoticed by the crowd that had come to welcome the Maharishi and bedeck him with floral garlands.

Krishnamurti would not exploit or be exploited by the counter-cultural and 'New Age' enthusiasms of the 1970s. If more people attended his talks and read his books, they did not get from them any confirmation of the then widely-held belief that a change was taking place in human consciousness, the spiritual dimension was being opened up and a new era of peace, love and caring was imminent. If Krishnamurti responded to the *Zeitgeist* at all, it was by becoming more vehement in his denunciation of gurus and the mentality of discipleship, and the teaching and practising of techniques of meditation. 'The gurus and religions have betrayed man,' he said in one talk in India, and even referred to some gurus having 'their own particular concentration camps.'[21] He saw no evidence of fundamental change, and maintained that belief in it was wishful thinking, blind to the manifest facts of what was happening in the world. In India, particularly, although multitudes of young Americans and Europeans flocked there in quest of the spiritual, he saw violence, greed, sectarianism, traditionalism and materialism threatening totally to swamp the religious spirit, as he had said they would forty years before in his conversation with Nehru.

Through Pupul Jayakar, who had been her close friend since childhood, Krishnamurti met Indira Gandhi, Nehru's daughter and the Indian Prime Minister since 1966. In the mid-1970s the political situation in India had become so potentially explosive, threatening anarchy and civil war, that Mrs Gandhi declared a State of Emergency. Opposition politicians were arrested and detained, and for over a year the Prime Minister was obliged by events to preside over a regime of repression. The situation was so bad that Krishnamurti cancelled his vist to India in 1975, on the grounds that he could not moderate what the teachings had to say on the subject of freedom and in the prevailing situation such talk could be politically inflammatory and might even land him in prison. The following year, however, he did go, Pupul Jayakar having secured Mrs Gandhi's assurance that he would be welcome and could speak freely. The Prime Minister sought private meetings with him, and they met twice. It was as a result of these meetings, she later told Pupul Jayakar, that although Krishnamurti had refused to tell her specifically what to do, she decided to lift the State of Emergency, release political prisoners and call elections. Krishnamurti was pleased when he heard the news, but asked, 'What will happen if she is defeated?'

She was, and soon afterwards was arrested, and although quickly released she was apprehensive about what her political enemies might contrive against her and her family. She continued the political struggle, however, and in 1978 was re-elected to Parliament, whereupon her enemies brought criminal charges against her, having her expelled and again briefly imprisoned.

Krishnamurti was in the country when she was released, and they met again. He urged her to leave politics, but this time she did not take his advice, saying that she knew that if she did not continue to fight she and her family would be destroyed. The following year there were elections again and she was returned as Prime Minister. Krishnamurti received the news of her success gravely, and told Pupul to stay close to her in the coming year as she would face great sorrow. Some months later her son Sanjay was killed in a flying accident, and the loss devastated her.

During her last term of prime ministerial office, Indira Gandhi and Krishnamurti developed a closer relationship, meeting whenever he was in India and often corresponding when he wasn't. During this time her political concerns broadened, and she publicly expressed apprehensions about the future of humanity that echoed those often expressed by Krishnamurti himself. She clearly drew moral and spiritual strength from his friendship and concern; she confided in him both her personal anguish and her despair as a politician with the escalation of sectarian conflict in the country. He was apprehensive about her safety and on one occasion he asked her if she was securely guarded. He saw for himself that she was when she paid a visit to him at the Rishi Valley school and the peaceful grounds swarmed incongruously with armed security men. But, in October 1984, she was assassinated by two of her security guards. One cannot but wonder whether Krishnamurti's question expressed a prescience.

Being a close observer of and personally involved in such events, Krishnamurti could hardly go along with the optimism about the dawning of a New Age, even if he was regarded by many as one of its heralds. He did, however, adopt one of the key words of the time, 'holistic', into his vocabulary, and he became profoundly interested in developments in science which supported the non-fragmentary view of the world. These developments were regarded by many as an exciting and revolutionary convergence of scientific and religious thought, and even potentially as catalysts of a radical change in human consciousness. Eminent scientists became his friends and participated in dialogues with him. Physicists' discoveries and theories about the ultimate nature of physical reality, and neurologists' discoveries about the functioning of the brain, particularly interested him. Developments in computer science and 'Artificial Intelligence' did, too. Where others saw a threat to humanity in these, he saw a challenge. The human brain, he said, was programmed like a computer, but was much less efficient and speedy in its operations, though it had a potential to function differently. Unless it fulfilled that potential it would become superseded by the computer and man would become an irrelevance, a superficial seeker after mere pleasure and entertainment.

In his eighties, Krishnamurti's mind was as alert as ever. He sought other minds to engage in dialogue, to explore and bring out further implications and relevances of the teachings. He continued, with unabated energy, his annual round of meetings and talks in England, Switzerland and the United States, even adding new venues, such as the Carnegie Hall in New York and the Barbican in London, to bring the teachings to a wider public. He also addressed specialist groups such as the scientists at Los Alamos and the politicians at the United Nations.

He existed to talk, he said, and when he ceased talking 'it would be over'. But he was frail, and the work took its toll. He once told his companion Mary Zimbalist, 'My life has been planned. It will tell me when to die.' In 1977 he had a prostate operation in Los Angeles, and after it he experienced what he later called 'a dialogue with death'. In great pain, he had a sense of dissociation from the body, which appeared to him to be floating in the air engaged in conversation with an entity that was a personification of death. Death pressed its demands with great insistence, but the body did not yield and it was helped in its resistance by a third entity, which was more powerful and vital than death itself. 'One felt very strongly and clearly', he said afterwards, 'that if the other had not interfered death would have won.' The experience was not an hallucination, he said. He was not delirious, his perceptions were perfectly clear; he simultaneously saw the drip-feed going into his body, rain on the window pane, Mary sitting close by and a nurse coming and going. Against this background the dialogue continued, eventually coming to the conclusion that 'the body would go on for many years, but death and the other would always be together until the organism could no longer be active'.[33]

In addition to talking to audiences and individuals, Krishnamurti was concerned in his last years to ensure that after his death the work of propagating the teachings and running the schools would continue. In addition to the schools there were

Krishnamurti Foundations in England, India and the United States, whose trustees had over the years worked at arranging the practical aspects of Krishnamurti's work – his itineraries, the preparation and publication of his books and the transcripts of the talks and dialogues. There had been dissensions within and between both the schools and the Foundations and he was anxious to see these resolved and to ensure that they did not recur. Many of the people who had participated in the work were getting on in years, so it was necessary to appoint younger people to positions of responsibility. He had frequent discussions with those who worked for the schools and Foundations, in which he expressed his concern that their work should continue to be imbued with the spirit of the teachings. As he put it at one meeting:

> Personally I think you are losing something marvellous if you reduce everything to producing books and keeping archives. When I am concerned about my intention for the Foundations, my wish is that the other thing, the flowering, should not wither away . . . My wish is that the perfume should be carried on.[33]

One way that 'the perfume' might be carried on, he conceived, was by establishing places where people could go to study and discuss the teachings in an appropriate environment. When a Swiss businessman, Friedrich Grohe, approached him in 1983 with a proposal to open a school in Switzerland, Krishnamurti suggested that instead he should finance the building of a study centre at Brockwood. Mr Grohe agreed. As in the past, whenever Krishnamurti conceived of a project which he believed important, somehow the funds were forthcoming to accomplish it. They were fortunate, too, in finding an architect who had specialized in the design of religious buildings and, moreover, was familiar with Krishnamurti's philosophy. Keith Critchlow produced a design which sensitively took account of both the site allocated for the Centre and its purpose as a place with a prevailing spiritual atmosphere, where people seriously concerned with the teachings could spend time studying them. Krishnamurti was keenly involved in all the stages of developing the project for the Centre, but regrettably did not live to see it open and operating.

Krishnamurti died on 17 February 1986, at Pine Cottage, Ojai. He was in his ninetieth year. Six weeks before, in Madras, he had given his last public talk, and at the conclusion of it he had said, in a barely audible voice, 'It ends.' Then he walked with friends on the beach at Adyar, where he had been 'discovered' seventy-six years before. The last talks were as vigorous and incisive as ever, but signs of rapid physical decline were apparent. It was imperative to get him to California, where he could have competent medical attention. There cancer of the pancreas was diagnosed. He suffered great pain during these last weeks, but remained clear-minded and coherent enough to discuss the work of the schools and Foundations and give instructions with regard to them. He also insisted that there should be no ceremony following his death, no business of people coming to 'salute the body'. The body, he instructed, should be simply cremated, and the ashes divided to be scattered equally at Ojai, Brockwood, and in the Ganges, at Rajghat. There were to be no memorials to him, no sanctity about the places associated with him. He and the body had served their purpose and were dispensable.

The teachings remained, and with regard to them he had said during one of his last talks in India:

> When K goes, as he must go, what will happen to the teaching? Will it go as the Buddha's teachings, which have been corrupted? You know what is happening; will the same fate await K's teaching? ... It depends upon you – how you limit it, how you think about it, what it means to you. If it means nothing except words, then it will go the way of the rest. If it means something very deep to you, to you personally, then it won't be corrupted. So it is up to you, not up to the Foundations and information centres and all the rest of that business. It depends upon you, whether you live the teachings or not.[25]

6

The Poet of Awareness

APART from the schools and Foundations, Krishnamurti's legacy to the world, and the chief repository of the teachings, is in the books published under his name. He actually wrote comparatively little, most of the books being transcripts of his talks and discussions, but as a young man he wrote some poetry, and from time to time throughout his life he recorded his experiences, observations and meetings with people in notebooks. These writings are distinguished by a totality of awareness and an economy and felicity in rendering it in words that merit their being regarded as literature, and Krishnamurti as a prose-poet of a high order. They are intimate and private writings, not addressed to an audience, and not seeking any effects. They give us a unique insight into the mind and daily life of Krishnamurti, as well as intimations as to what certain terms which he commonly used, such as 'choiceless awareness', 'negative sensitivity', and 'perception unpolluted by thought', really mean – or rather what it is like to be in the states of consciousness that they describe.

'I am not a poet,' Krishnamurti wrote in the foreword to his book *The Song of Life* in 1931, 'I have merely tried to put into words the manner of my realisation.' Despite the disclaimer, the words in which he expressed 'the manner of his realisation' sometimes condensed and structured meaning in the way that only poetry can. For example:

> I have lived the good and evil of men,
> And dark became the horizon of my love.
> I have known the morality and immorality of men,
> And cruel became my anxious thought.
> I have shared in the piety and impiety of Men,

> And heavy became the burden of life.
> I have pursued the race of the ambitious,
> And vain became the glory of life.
> And now I have fathomed the secret purpose of desire.

This poem is exceptional in its conciseness, and, significantly, is one of the last he wrote. Others in the same volume, and in the 1928 volume *The Immortal Friend*, are more loosely structured and employ more conventional poetic imagery and locutions. His *Song of Love*, for example, begins:

> Oh! Listen,
> I will sing to you the song of my Beloved.
> Where the soft green slopes of the still mountains
> Meet the blue shimmering waters of the noisy sea,
> Where the bubbling brook shouts in ecstasy,
> Where the still pools reflect the calm heavens,
> There thou wilt meet with my Beloved.
> In the vale where the cloud hangs in loneliness
> Searching the mountain for rest,
> In the still smoke climbing heavenwards,
> In the hamlet toward the setting sun,
> In the thin wreaths of the fast disappearing clouds,
> There thou wilt meet with my Beloved.

It is arguably appropriate that a 'song of love' should be expansive and exuberant, and there is no doubt that this and other early poems express a genuine ecstatic, even mystical, experience, and are therefore interesting for what they have to tell us about 'the manner of his realisation'. On the whole, though, they are too undisciplined (nine adjectives in the first four lines above, not one of them surprising) and too laden with poeticisms really to succeed as poetry. In the last analysis we have to agree with Krishnamurti that he wasn't a poet, at least at the time when he wrote his verse compositions, even if in those compositions poetical feeling abounds.

In the mature Krishnamurti philosophy, feeling is regarded equally as subversive as thought to the direct perception of 'what is'. Thought and feeling are both of the ego, pleasurable because they confirm the continuity of the self. They are at once reinforced and circumscribed by past experience, which inhibits present experiencing. But what, we ask, can perception divested of thought and feeling, or experiencing unencumbered by past experience, be like? Well, that is something we learn from poetry, though few poets express it more than sporadically, and some, like Wordsworth, have written fine poetry lamenting the loss of that mode of perception. William Blake sustained it longer than most, and perhaps the reason he did so is explained in his lines:

> He who bends to himself a joy
> Does the winged life destroy;
> But he who kisses the joy as it flies
> Lives in eternity's sunrise.

We try to 'bend to ourselves' our joys by investing them with feeling, entangling them with thought, slotting them into memory in the expectation that they will retain their magic upon retrieval or carry some of it over to make future joys more joyous. But they don't, because the mind and the ego are involved, and experience negates experiencing. For experiencing to occur, experience must be set aside. This is Krishnamurti's 'living and dying from moment to moment', which equates with Blake's 'living in eternity's sunrise'. This is what gives his later writings, in the *Notebook*, their poetic quality. He 'kisses the joy as it flies', but doesn't hold on to it, over-embellish it with words or dwell on it overlong, but just sets it down, distinctly and precisely, and lets it go.

A passage from *Krishnamurti's Notebook*, will illustrate the point. Shall it be a description of dawn in the Swiss mountains, of a sunset in India, of the behaviour of three crows in a tree, of a lily-pond, of a huge rock and the effects of changing light upon it, of the river Ganges and its human, animal and bird life, of a child throwing a stick, of two old women weeding a garden, or of a young village woman walking along a road behind her husband engulfed in an 'impenetrable sadness'? Krishnamurti observed the life of nature and of man with equal clarity and sensitivity. The following passage is chosen because it combines both:

> The sun was behind the clouds and the flat lands stretched far into the horizon which was turning golden brown and red . . . There was an intensity and a sweeping dignity and delight in the earth itself and in the common things that one passed every day. The canal, a long narrow strip of water of melting fire, went north and south among the rice fields, silent and lonely; there was not much traffic on it; there were barges, crudely made, with square or triangular sails, carrying firewood or sand and men sitting huddled together, looking very grave. The palm trees dominated the wide green earth; they were of every shape and size, independent and carefree, swept by the winds

and burnt by the sun. The rice fields were ripening golden yellow and there were largish white birds among them, their wings lazily beating the air. Bullock carts, carrying casuarina firewood to the town, went by, a long line of them, creaking and the men walking and the load was heavy. It was none of these common sights that made the evening enchanting; they were all part of the fading evening, the noisy buses, the silent bicycles, the croaks of the frogs, the smell of the evening. There was a deep widening immensity, an imminent clarity of that otherness, with its impenetrable strength and purity. What was beautiful was now glorified in splendour; everything was clothed in it; there was ecstasy and laughter not only deeply within but among the palms and rice fields. Love is not a common thing but it was there in the hut with an oil lamp; it was with that old woman, carrying something heavy on her head; with that naked boy, swinging on a piece of string a piece of wood which gave out many sparks for it was his fireworks. It was everywhere, so common that you could pick it up under a dead leaf or in that jasmine by the old crumbling house. It was there filling your heart, your mind and the sky; it remained and would never leave you. Only you would have to die to everything, without roots, without a tear. Then it would come to you, if you were lucky and you forever ceased to run after it, begging, hoping, crying ... It would be there, on that dusty, dark road.[16]

Krishnamurti's prose does not read as if it has been worked at, or as if there has been any pondering over the most effective word or image. It is observation set down spontaneously and simply, even carelessly. The writing as such – the vocabulary, syntax and style – does not draw attention to itself. It is at the eye's service, not the mind's; it is transparent, we see the world through it. An artist could paint pictures just working from Krishnamurti's descriptions; they convey such a precise and vital sense of 'being there'. At the same time they convey something else. They not only show 'what is', they illuminate it; or, more precisely, they show that 'what is' is itself luminous, glorious, resplendent, vital; and that to the eye that really sees, the vision uncluttered by thought and feeling, every act of perception discloses 'the miracle of the new'.

If the works of artists, in the literary or any other medium, are artefacts, things-in-themselves, ordered constructs wrested from a world of disorder, as prevailing artistic theory maintains, then Krishnamurti was not an artist. He did not create in this sense. Nor would he have wished to. 'Creation', he wrote,

> is not for the talented, for the gifted; they only know creativeness but never creation. Creation is beyond thought and image, beyond the word and expression. It is not to be communicated for it cannot be

formulated, it cannot be wrapped up in words. It can be felt in complete awareness. It cannot be used and put on the market, to be haggled over and sold.[16]

Creation is 'the miracle of the new' disclosing itself in 'what is' in any moment of time that will never be again. Man may participate in it, but he cannot appropriate it; he may observe it, even describe it, but however well he does so the description will remain something else in its own right, for 'the word is not the thing'.

It was his sense of the marvellousness and immensity of creation that made Krishnamurti indifferent to most of the artistic creations of human beings, including his own writings, but at the same time it is this sense that imbues some of his passages with a marvellousness of their own. An experience he often refers to in his *Notebook* and *Journal* is what he calls 'the benediction'. Other writers have spoken of similar experiences: one thinks of James Joyce's 'epiphanies', of W. B. Yeats's moments when 'I was blessed and could bless', R. M. Bucke's 'cosmic consciousness'. But Krishnamurti's 'benediction' is more than a heightened state of consciousness. It is something in the manner of a visitation:

> Quietly it came, so gently that one was not aware of it, so close to the earth, among the flowers. It was spreading, covering the earth and one was in it, not as an observer but of it.[16]

It is not a subjective experience; other people can be involved in it:

> Yesterday, as we were walking up a beautiful narrow valley, its steep sides dark with pines and green fields full of wild flowers, suddenly, most unexpectedly, for we were talking of other things, a benediction descended upon us, like gentle rain. We became the centre of it. It was gentle, pressing, infinitely tender and peaceful, enfolding us in a power that was beyond all fault and reason.[16]

Sometimes he speaks of it as a 'presence': 'That presence is here, filling the room, spilling over the hills, beyond the waters, covering the earth.' And: 'It's here, there's a beauty and a glory and a sense of wordless ecstasy.'[16]

There is poetry in Krishnamurti's descriptions of 'the benediction', and they give us an idea of the quality of the poetry of his other writings. It is a poetry not so much of a heightened as of a total consciousness, not of ecstatic transports but of a down-to-earth, all-embracing awareness. It is a characteristic of Krishnamurti's writings that there is a transition from the poetry of description to the poetry of statement or reflection, as in the long passage quoted above when he begins to write about love, but the transition is not abrupt or arbitrary. The statement is not something cunningly superimposed on the narrative in the manner of a preacher's lesson, but something enfolded in it that grows out from it, as the totality of the writer's consciousness embraces 'what is' simultaneously on the levels of physical and metaphysical reality. When he writes that 'love ... was there in the hut with the oil lamp', the statement is no more fanciful than 'the canal went north and south among the rice fields'. He never modifies his descriptions with the word 'seemed' or compromises his vision with any suggestion that there may be different kinds or orders of truth. The world disclosed by 'the benediction' is not some other world overlying the mundane, it is integral with the mundane, always there if not always seen or sensed; statements about it are not equivocal or indulgences of some 'poetic licence' with truth, they are as true and literal as any other statements about 'what is'. The benediction literally discloses reality, in the sense of making manifest that which is closed off and hidden from the partial and limited awareness that human beings accept as normal.

Krishnamurti's total awareness extended also to psychological perception. His descriptions, in the three volumes of his *Commentaries on Living* and in *The Only Revolution*, of people he met or who came to him for counsel or to discuss things, are always penetrating and succinct. Gestures, facial expressions, 'body language', tones of voice, things said and unsaid, all come under his scrutiny. Unerringly he sees through pretences, protestations, bogus sincerities and all the conscious and unconscious stratagems that people employ to deceive themselves and others. Of a woman who came to listen to one of his talks 'in case the teacher of teachers spoke', he observed:

> She was big and soft-spoken; but there lurked condemnation, nourished by her convictions and beliefs. She was suppressed and hard, but had given herself over to brotherhood and its good cause. She added that she would know when the teacher spoke, for she and her group had some mysterious way of knowing it, which was not given to others. The pleasure of exclusive knowledge was so obvious in the way she said it, in the gesture and the tilt of the head.[3]

Of another young woman, a dancer, who came to see him 'to talk about beauty and the spirit', he observed:

> She must have felt proud of her art, for there was arrogance about her, not only the arrogance of achievement but also that of some inner

recognition of her spiritual worth. As another would be satisfied with outward success, she was gratified by her spiritual advancement . . . She had jewels on, and her nails were red; her lips were painted the appropriate colour . . . Vanity and ambition were on her face; she wanted to be known both spiritually and as an artist, and now the spirit was gaining.[3]

Many self-professed spiritual seekers and religious men sought Krishnamurti out, and while they talked about themselves, their problems and aspirations, he observed them:

> He was very rich man; he was lean and hard, but had an easy air with a ready smile. He was now looking across the valley, but the quickening beauty had not touched him; there was no softening of the face, the lines were still hard and determined. He was still hunting, not for money, but for what he called God.[3]

Another God-seeker, rather proud of his disciplined religious observances, comes under scrutiny:

> Obstinacy of purpose and absence of pliability were shown in the way he held his body. He was obviously driven by an extraordinarily powerful will, and though he smiled easily his will was ever on the alert, watchful and dominant . . . He had a gentle side, too, for he would look at the lawn and the gay flowers, and smile . . . If beauty fitted into the pattern of his purpose, he would accept it; but there always lurked the fear of sensuality, whose ache he tried to contain.[3]

Deft and perceptive pen-portraits such as these abound in Krishnamurti's writings, revealing him as a shrewd observer of people as well as a sensitive and passionate observer of the natural world. Add to these qualities the simple eloquence of his writings on life and philosophy, many of which are masterpieces in the art of the essay, and we have an *œuvre* which, in the vigour and clarity of its language and the freshness and originality of its observations and insights, yields in abundance the delights, surprises and revelations that are the stuff of enduring literature.

7

The Mystery

WHO or what was Krishnamurti? Although he repudiated the role of holy man, one cannot read his biographies or the memoirs of those who knew him without gathering the impression that he was not an ordinary man. That the pompous and pretentious Leadbeater should have picked him out for the quasi-divine role of the World Teacher is a fact beyond comprehension. Reason balks at the idea of any transcendent Power or Intelligence encumbering its messenger with such a dubious mystagogue as his promoter; unless we suppose that that Intelligence is endowed with an ironic sense of humour. The boy transported from the beach at Adyar to be nurtured for such an august pre-ordained role should in all probability have turned out either a coterie-guru with feet of clay indiscernible only to his devotees, or a fairly unexceptional human being compelled by his reason and passion to repudiate his role in the interests of being human. Instead the improbable boy turned out to be – well, a world teacher. We can remove the definite article and the capitals, but to shed the term of its Theosophical pretensions does not shed light on the mystery of Krishnamurti. That there was something about him, something that manifested in his presence, that certainly manifested in the eloquence of many of his unprepared talks, some unique power or energy that he emanated, is attested by many people who knew or met him. He may have regarded the holy man role as adopted by fashionable gurus as a masquerade, although one sometimes suspects that by playing down his exceptionality he was something of a masquerader himself. Clearly, to have allowed himself to be worshipped would have been incompatible with the teaching, but equally clearly there was something about him that people could not help holding in awe or reverence. And he was aware of it; in fact he was as puzzled as others were by the mystery of who he was. Self-knowledge he undoubtedly had, but the teachings did not emanate from the known self. To profess to know their provenance, to attribute them to 'the Masters' or to God, would be to tie them into something too specific, and to encourage their acceptance or rejection for the wrong reasons. He simply saw no point in dwelling on the mystery, just as he saw no point in performing spiritual healings, although he could do so. Miracles, he said, 'are fascinating child's play ... I hold that no great Teacher would perform a miracle, because that would be a betrayal of the Truth.'[33]

He would talk about the mystery with friends, however, just as he would sometimes perform a healing upon a friend. In 1934 he wrote to Lady Emily Lutyens, who had expressed disappointment that he had denied being the World Teacher: 'I have only said that it doesn't matter who or what I am but that they should examine what I say, which does not mean that I have denied being the World Teacher.'[33] Some forty years later, in conversation with Mary Lutyens, his biographer, he talked about himself and the teaching, saying:

> Here is the phenomenon of this chap who isn't trained, who has no discipline. How did he get all this? What is it? If it were only K – he is uneducated, gentle – so where does it come from? This person hasn't thought out the teaching ... It is like – what is the biblical term? – revelation. It happens all the time when I'm talking.[33]

We recall his descriptions, in the *Notebook*, of his experiences of 'the benediction' and of the presence of sacredness. He also spoke sometimes about an awareness of being protected. He had no sense of self-importance, but he had an ever-present certainty that his mind and body were in service to something beyond and that his tenure of them was in the nature of a trust. 'The body is here to talk,' he said. 'Anything else is irrelevant, so the body has to be protected ... [and] I feel there is another kind of protection that is not mine.'[33] In this context he sometimes spoke of 'the power', for instance, 'the power must have watched over this body from the moment it was born.' He would not, of course, personify 'the power', for he saw that was the mistake the religions had made, and his references to it were more matter-of-fact than pious. 'That thing is in the room,' he would say, and others would be aware of the presence too. But he would not or could not be more specific.

'I can't look behind the curtain,' he said.

His self-effacingness was ambiguous, however, because sometimes he spoke as if he were putting himself on a par with the greatest religious teachers. One has to bear in mind that even though Krishnamurti was aware of himself as the exemplar of the teachings he knew that they were not his creation, and so could speak quite objectively about himself. In discussion with members of the Krishnamurti Foundation he once said:

> If people come here and ask, 'What was it like to live with this man?' would you be able to convey it to them? If any of the Buddha's disciples were alive would not one travel to the ends of the earth to see them, to find out from them what it had been like to live in his presence?[33]

And to Mary Lutyens he said:

> The Buddha went through all that, the suffering etc., then threw it aside and became enlightened. What he taught was original but he went through all that. But here is a freak who didn't go through any of it. Jesus may have been a freak too.[33]

He never drew such parallels in his public talks, but with friends, who knew him to be the most unassuming of human beings and whom he could trust not to misconstrue him, he could speak more freely. Everyone knew that he was not promoting himself as a Bodhisattva or Messiah, but they also knew that such comparisons might not be entirely inapt: the uniqueness both of the teachings and of the man himself invited them. That uniqueness, though, was part of the problem. When Krishnamurti referred to himself as a 'freak' he was not being funny or self-deprecating. He sometimes qualified the term, saying 'biological freak', referring to 'the process' that he had undergone at various times in his life, and he expressed concern that his very uniqueness might invalidate the teachings, for 'if a thing is unique then others cannot get it'. His fundamental conviction, though, was that others could get it, that the teaching in its simplicity, rationality and coherence was truth unadorned and demystified, and that if he had to be something of a freak to convey it, that was really irrelevant. As he put it: 'The freak was kept for the teaching, but the freak is totally unimportant.'[33]

Mary Zimbalist, Krishnamurti's closest companion throughout the last two decades of his life, says that he would sometimes tell her, minutes before beginning to address one of the vast audiences that congregated to hear him, that he had no idea what he was going to talk about. He would sit before an audience, whether of tens or of thousands of people, for maybe two or three minutes before starting to talk, then proceed without hesitation. Aldous Huxley said that to hear him 'was like listening to a discourse of the Buddha – such power, such intrinsic authority'.[33] Where did the words, the teaching, come from? Krishnamurti always said that his mind was 'a vacancy', and he asked, 'was vacancy necessary for this [the teaching] to manifest?' He thought that it probably was necessary: 'That thing must have said, "There must be vacancy or I – it – cannot function." . . . So what is *that* that keeps it vacant in order to say all these things? Did it find a boy that was most likely to remain vacant?'[33] He raises the questions but cannot answer them. All he can say is that when he talks out of that vacancy, 'it is like revelation'. The teaching 'comes out without my thinking about it, it becomes logical, rational. If I think it out carefully, write it down, repeat it, nothing happens.'[33]

'Revelation' always lays claim to special authority because it purports to come from beyond the mind of the human being who channels it, but so varied and inconsistent is the literature of revelation, from the canonical, biblical and koranic texts to modern pseudo-Bibles like *The Book of Mormon* and *The Oahpse*, that the mystery of the provenance of the material obviously cannot be taken as any guarantee to its truth. Of course, Krishnamurti never stated publicly that the teachings were revelation, nor did he seek to invest them with authority by reference to their source: that would have been to invite the uncritical cultic adherence that he regarded as the enemy of truth. Only with his intimates did he speak of revelation and discuss the mystery of how the teachings came into being, as it were through him. Was it perhaps analogous to artistic creation at the highest level, the level of his favourite composers, Mozart and Beethoven? 'Does this thing that manifests come out of a universal pool,' he asked, 'as genius comes out of it in other fields?' He was dubious about this explanation, though, for 'with artists and poets it is different because they build up to it', and anyway 'the religious spirit has nothing to do with genius'.[33] One might query his rejection of the analogy, however, particularly with the example of Mozart, who said that his compositions came to him *in toto* in his head and he just wrote them down. But the comparison is suggestive rather than explanatory; one mystery doesn't really throw light on another. It is, though, more apt than to compare Krishnamurti's teachings with the literature of religious revelation. If Krishnamurti was a 'channel', he was not one given to ecstatic transports, possession, or trance states in which normal consciousness is suspended, and if his 'vacancy' was somehow annexed when he talked or wrote, it was not by some superhuman or transmundane entity that couched its message to mankind in symbolism or parable. Both the teachings and the manner in which they were conveyed are entirely rational, just as the music of Mozart is rational. Also, like the music, they are so simple and direct that they impress initially not by virtue of their originality but by their inevitability and truth. Great works of art have this quality of inevitability, of being not something created but something revealed; and that something has nothing to do with the life or personality of the artist. The analogy does hold, up to a point. Perhaps it is relevant to take it a bit further, to consider that to seek beyond Krishnamurti for the provenance of the teachings may be as futile an enterprise as to seek beyond Mozart for the source of the Jupiter symphony.

With artists, poets and composers there is often a discrepancy between the life and the work, even to the extent that the work may embody order and perfection whereas the life is conspicuous only for its mess and confusion. There is a Romantic psychology of art which regards the work as something achieved in spite of or by way of compensation for the inadequacies and imperfections of the artist, or as the sublimation of intractable psychic discord. The more conspicuous the discrepancy between the life and the work, the more readily is the accolade of 'genius' bestowed. It was probably with awareness of this view in mind that Krishnamurti said that 'the religious spirit has nothing to do with genius'. In his own case, although there was a striking difference between Krishnamurti the man in the world and Krishnamurti the teacher, the two were not discrepant or incompatible. He had human idiosyncracies that the puritanical might consider inappropriate in a spiritual being: a taste for quality cars and clothes (he always visited his Savile Row tailor when in London), an interest in things mechanical, a boyish enjoyment of adventure and thriller movies, novels, and silly jokes, and, when he was a young man, a fondness for playing golf. In social situations he was diffident, even seemingly shy, rarely initiating or participating in conversations. But it would be a cavilling spirit that would reprehend these human characteristics as inconsistencies unworthy of the great religious teacher, and in fact they are entirely consistent with his statements that when he was not engaged in talking or writing, when 'that thing' that manifested through him was not present, his mind was in abeyance and vacant.

Krishnamurti preferred to regard his exceptionality as analogous to that of the discoverer or pioneer rather than the artistic genius. The problem that most people have with the teaching is that it appears to demand a commitment as total and uncompromising as Krishnamurti's own, and even a like 'vacancy' of mind, which he admitted was an innate characteristic and not something he achieved or induced. That we should be like him is a requirement as difficult to fulfil as St Paul's injunction, 'Be ye therefore perfect, even as your Father in Heaven is perfect.' In response to this objection Krishnamurti said on one occasion, 'We don't all have to be Edisons to turn on the electric light', and on another, 'Christopher Columbus went to America in a sailing ship; we can go by jet.'[33] One cannot but feel that the analogies are somewhat inapt – it is never going to be that easy – but they do make the point that we don't have to be 'freaks' to benefit from the teachings.

There is a theory that once something has been done or a skill has been developed by one or several members of a species, others are able to do it much more easily. The theory was proposed by Dr Rupert Sheldrake in *A New Science of Life* (1980)[45], as a development of his 'hypothesis of formative causation', which holds that form in chemical and biological structures is determined by a 'morphogenetic field'. This is immaterial and non-energetic but works in synchrony with energy factors to specify structural singularities. Sheldrake cites the observed fact that chemists often have difficulty crystallizing newly synthesized substances, but once crystallization has taken place in one laboratory it tends to do so more easily in others. He proposes that there is a principle of 'morphic resonance' at work, and that this resonance builds up cumulatively so that when new structures are generated their forms are determined by the past forms of structures with the same components. In respect of behaviour, the theory proposes that learned behaviours are reinforced in species by morphic resonance. Furthermore, because this resonance is non-energetic and therefore not diminished by travelling through space, it is possible that increased facility in learning and the exercise of newly learned skills should manifest in different members, or groups, of a species in widely separated locations without there being any mode of physical communication between them. This phenomenon has been observed, for instance, in laboratory rats developing maze-running skills.

Sheldrake's theory is summarized because when someone brought it to Krishnamurti's attention he showed great interest in it. It supported what he was suggesting by his Columbus analogy: that what the pioneer does may be extremely arduous and demand exceptional abilities, but once he has done it the task becomes easier for others. It also suggested that change or learning could be effected by a non-specific and immaterial influence. In his later discussions with David Bohm, Krishnamurti said several times that if ten people fundamentally changed and really lived according to the teachings, the effect they would have on the world would be tremendous and revolutionary. When Bohm asked him if he was suggesting that 'there is some sort of extra-sensory effect that spreads', he confirmed that that was exactly what he meant.[22] It was his conviction that the immense energy and intelligence of 'that thing' which manifested through him, that he and others sometimes felt as a tremendous physical presence, could not be limited or contained but simply must have an effect upon the world, an effect maybe more direct and pervasive than the teachings as communicated in his talks and books.

In that case, Krishnamurti was something more than a mouthpiece for the teachings, or a pioneer and examplar of a psycho-spiritual revolution. Although he considered the enigma of his origins and his identity irrelevant to the truth of the teachings, he was intrigued when, in 1985, a renowned Buddhist scholar in India told him that in a very early Tibetan manuscript he had come across a prediction that the Lord Maitreya would be incarnated in a being with the name Krishnamurti. The scholar had volunteered the information very hesitantly, with a sense of awe and reverence, and he was non-committal when asked if he really believed in the prediction and its fulfilment. Krishnamurti himself told Mary Zimbalist that he was 'very sceptical' about it, but he was apparently impressed by the sincerity and the content of the Pandit's communication. No doubt both his scepticism and his interest were attributable to the fact that if it were true it would prove Leadbeater, Mrs Besant and the Theosophical tradition right after all. But he told Mary Lutyens, 'The Maitreya is too concrete, not subtle enough', meaning presumably that it was a concept overloaded with religious and mystical significance but lacking vitality. Probably the most revealing statement we have of his own view of himself is the one he recorded in the presence of one or two of his closest friends just a few days before his death. Speaking with an effort and slowly, in a weak voice but with intense emphasis, he said:

> For seventy years that super energy – no – that immense energy, immense intelligence, has been using this body. I don't think people realise what tremendous energy and intelligence went through this body – there's a twelve-cylinder engine ... And after seventy years the body can't stand it – can't stand any more ... You won't find another body like this, or that supreme intelligence operating in a body, for many hundred years. You won't see it again. When he goes, it goes. There is no consciousness left behind of *that* consciousness, of *that* state. They'll all pretend to try to imagine they can get in touch with that. Perhaps they will somewhat if they live the teachings. But nobody has done it. Nobody. And so that's that.[34]

So, unequivocally at the end, Krishnamurti seemed to confess an awareness of his uniqueness, despite the fact that he had often said that if something is unique it is meaningless. We note, though, that it is to the body that this quality of uniqueness is attributed; perhaps a distinction has to be made between the body that was a vehicle for the communication of the teachings and the body that lived in accordance with them. Certain disciplines of the body, in the interests of maintaining the vitality, clarity, sensitivity and energy of the mind, are enjoined by the teachings, but presumably not everyone has to undergo the physical and mental rigours of 'the process'. As he said, we don't all have to be Edisons. But even so, as those last words indicate, his seventy-year-long ministry in the world apparently did not fundamentally change anybody. In the end there were not ten or even one or two spirits to bring to bear a palpable psychic influence. It would be wrong, though, to construe his words, 'And so that's that', as expressing disappointment, or even resignation, for Krishnamurti never entertained hopes or expectations, nor did he consider that what he did could be faulted or vindicated by results. The words expressed, rather, a clear-sighted recognition of fact. He had done what he had to do in the world, and in the body of the teachings, together with the schools and Foundations, he left behind a substantial legacy. If nobody yet has lived the teachings so completely as to become like him, there are many people who, through exposure to them, have not been the same afterwards. There are a few who, having been close to him in life and inspired by the truth and radiance of the man, as well as of the teachings, remain dedicated to the task of continuing his work, in the sense of keeping the schools and Foundations going.

It could not have been otherwise. If anyone embodied the teachings in his or her life as fully as Krishnamurti did himself, that person would not necessarily be a conspicuous participant in the ongoing work associated with his name. Krishnamurti was well aware of the dangers inherent in the idea of an apostolic succession; he specifically said that he wanted none of that. Nobody, he said, should set himself up after his death as an authority on, or interpreter of, the teachings. The Foundations should be religious centres, not in the sense of having some kind of 'holy' atmosphere, but places where 'a flame is living, not the ashes of it'. They should be places where people could light their own candle from that flame and could go to study, discuss or live the teachings in an appropriate environment.

Krishnamurti's injunction against interpretation might appear to imply a censure of anything written about the teachings, and the present author has not been unmindful of it. But Krishnamurti certainly did not mean to imply that the teachings should be accorded scriptural infallibility or regarded as sacrosanct statements of revealed truth. He also said: 'Discuss, criticise, go into it. Read K's books and intellectually tear them to pieces. Or intellectually go with it. Discuss. That's not interpretation.'[34] It is in this spirit that the following chapters are written.

PART TWO

•

The Message

8

On Human Bondage

To propose to set man free is a fine declaration of purpose for a philosopher, but not a particularly original one. Political philosophers from Rousseau to Mill and Marx, existentialists from Kierkegaard to Sartre, and even the linguistic philosopher Wittgenstein, who said his aim was 'to show the fly the way out of the fly-bottle', have all proposed a purpose similar to that declared by Krishnamurti in 1929. Where all philosophers of freedom differ, however, is in their ideas of human bondage, and it is in this respect that Krishnamurti's thinking is more radical than other philosophers', and utterly original.

Political philosophers generally take the view that human freedom is necessarily limited. The social contract is an agreement to surrender a portion of one's freedom in exchange for the benefits and satisfactions of living in an ordered society. This exchange is regarded as a civilized arrangement, for the freedom we have to surrender in order to cement the social contract is the freedom to gratify such things as our selfish, acquisitive, vengeful or lustful impulses. We are on the whole pleased to have these impulses in ourselves and others constrained by the authority and power vested, by virtue of the social contract, in the law and its custodians. But the question of where precisely the limits of the rightful exercise of this authority and power lie is a vexed one. People tend to have different ideas about it, depending on whether they take the view that human nature is inherently good or inherently evil, and also depending on whether they themselves wield power and authority or have it wielded over them. In as much as people have different ideas about the subject, different structures of power and authority exist in different human societies; these differences give rise to conflict, envy, ideology, persecution, politics and power-seeking. No wonder people come to the conclusion that the very idea of the social contract is unworkable, seeking to opt out of it, either by fighting their way to the top of the heap, where they can do as they like, or by trying to reclaim their liberties by becoming self-governing and self-sufficient in as many aspects of life as possible.

Philosophers have discussed at length the pros and cons of such opting out, but it was left to Krishnamurti to point out that the fundamental reason why the social contract is unworkable is not that people misconstrue or contravene its terms, but that the very idea of the voluntary surrender of freedom is a myth. This is because the people who constitute our societies do not have any freedom to surrender: the basic cause of their troubles and those of the world is precisely this lack of freedom, this condition of bondage, which for the most part they are unaware of.

It has been observed often enough that revolutions in human societies have only produced a reshuffling of the hierarchy, a new ruling élite – and in the course of time, in all but superficial effects, a restoration of the *status quo ante*. This tendency of human societies, whatever upheavals they may undergo, to stabilize along the lines of a rather predictable pattern – moreover a pattern which is the antithesis of the declared aims of most well-meaning revolutionaries – testifies to the existence of some intractable element in those societies. As societies are assemblies of human individuals, it is probable that the intractable element is to be found in the individual. Could it be that, whatever they may profess, people do not really want freedom, or that they fear it?

From Dostoevsky to Erich Fromm, writers have argued that this is the case, and it is difficult to deny the proposition in the face of their evidence. But Krishnamurti points to another factor in the situation: that to be conscious of freedom negates the condition. As he put it: 'If one says "I am free", then one is not free.'[9] This paradox takes us to the heart of Krishnamurti's concept of man, mind and consciousness, and we shall come back to it. However, there is another paradox to note here: that although freedom is negated by our becoming conscious of it, it is by being conscious and aware of the modes of bondage that circumscribe and delimit our lives that we make possible the experience of true freedom. In this context we must not speak of the achievement of freedom because, according to Krishnamurti, freedom is not something that can be achieved, for in seeking to achieve something there is an element of time – the idea that something *is not* but *will be* – and there is dualism and conflict because the person conceives simultaneously an actual and ideal state. All these things negate true freedom.

It might be objected that Krishnamurti set up a criterion of freedom which disqualifies from the condition all but a few rare souls such as himself. To read him on the subject is to apprehend a clearer recognition of one's own unfreedom, which may give rise to feelings of dismay or acquiescence. On the other hand, in that recognition there must be, for some, a stimulus towards personal change and growth, the shedding of some elements of inauthenticity in their lives and the establishment of a degree more integrity, or wholeness of being. Krishnamurti himself would not allow that authenticity, wholeness and freedom come by degrees, although it is surely the case that he is not so widely read for the transformation that his teaching induces as for the insights it gives. His perceptions of the varieties of human bondage are sometimes surprising.

'To be free,' he wrote, 'is not merely to do what you like, or to break away from outward circumstances, but to understand the whole problem of dependence.'[6] Or again: 'Freedom implies the total abnegation and denial of all inward psychological authority.'[11] Now, the idea that authority constrains individual freedom is clear enough, but we generally tend to think of that authority as something imposed, working from without. The idea of the existence of an 'inward psychological authority' dictating our behaviour and our thinking, even determining what we feel, see and experience, is another matter. Of course, it is not an entirely unfamiliar concept. Modern psychological and sociological studies have shown clearly that the techniques of conditioning, 'thought reform' and 'behaviour modification' can plant in an individual an inward determining authority which directs his thinking and behaviour when he imagines that he is exercising his own free will. The cynical and exploitative use of such techniques has provoked many protests about the erosion of liberties and about the ethical implications of meddling with the human mind. But the problem goes deeper than that, for conditioning begins in infancy: all the traditions, beliefs, ideas, even the language that we acquire from our social and cultural background, only serve to constitute that inward psychological authority which keeps us in bondage.

'To see, you must be free from all authority, tradition, fear, and thought with its cunning words,'[8] wrote Krishnamurti. The conventional wisdom regards man's development of language and rational thought as a glorious and evolutionary thing, but Krishnamurti regarded these faculties with profound circumspection, for he saw them as a root cause of human bondage.

> We are lost, we are forlorn because we have accepted words, words, words ... You may give significance to life, you can invent as philosophers and theoreticians do, as religious people do – invent the significance of life – that is their job, but this is feeding on words when you need substance; you are fed with words, and you are satisfied with words.[13]

Such satisfaction, he implies, is inauthentic living, it is living in bondage, for the word is not the reality; the reality lies beyond the reach of words. It lies in simply seeing and experiencing, without allowing what is seen and experienced to be dwelt on by thought or interpreted by words. True freedom exists only in the moments of such seeing and experiencing.

Thought is the real villain and tyrant in Krishnamurti's view of human bondage. One of his books is entitled *Freedom From the Known*, which expresses one of his most difficult propositions: that knowledge, which is based upon thought, is bondage. The proposition is difficult because it is virtually axiomatic in our thinking that knowledge liberates. However, if you equate freedom with authentic and fresh seeing and experiencing, as Krishnamurti did, you can see how acquired knowledge and the processes of thought can diminish or even negate that authenticity and freshness.

Time has to be brought into the discussion, too, because knowledge is acquired in time. It depends on time because it is sustained by memory, which is the repository of things past; also rational, linear thought goes on in time. Acquired knowledge and experience constitute one of the several kinds of inward psychological authority which limit our freedom, for they make us insensible to the new. The mind is burdened by the past, by expectations which are based on past experience, sustained by memory, and, so burdened, it is not free.

Memory, the past, expectation and thought are all involved in a form of human bondage that anybody will acknowledge as such: fear. Fear arises when the pain and suffering of yesterday are carried over by thought, and expectation, to tomorrow; it also arises when memory sustains and dwells on a pleasure or satisfaction and we fear losing it or not being able to enjoy it again; or when we contemplate what we are, what we have become in the course of time, and thought dwells on the vulnerability and ephemerality of this self which is a product of time and becoming. So pleasure, desire and death are things closely bound up with fear, and really to be free and to be without fear is not to be tyrannized by pleasure, desire and death.

Does this mean renouncing pleasure and desire, and suppressing them? This is what most religions have advocated, even demanded, of their devotees. But renunciation and suppression do not lead to freedom, they lead to psychological division, contradiction and struggle, and thus they perpetuate fear. Krishnamurti, who was not concerned with laying down codes of morality but with specifying the conditions of human freedom, did not teach renunciation and suppression. He proposed that by understanding the nature of pleasure and desire we might become free of their tyranny. Sensual pleasure, as a response to seeing or experiencing something beautiful, is a sensation which arises spontaneously and naturally; such a response does not pose a problem, nor does it constitute any form of bondage. But when thought comes in, giving rise to the desire to possess, to hold on to, to perpetuate, then the perfectly natural reaction is perverted; and in this way pleasure itself is vitiated by desire.

It is important in this context to distinguish between thought and intelligence. To understand all the modes of dependence that bind us, we need to exercise great intelligence. 'Can you find out whether you are free from authority?' Krishnamurti asked, and he warned that 'it needs tremendous inquiry into yourself, great awareness.[11]' The quality that characterizes the truly liberated mind is that of 'choiceless awareness'. Awareness arises in the exercise of intelligence, but choosing is a function of thought. If, recognizing that desire is bondage, you choose and resolve not to desire something, what situation is created? Necessarily, it is a situation of conflict, because you have divided yourself into two persons, the one who desires and the one that vetoes the desire: inward division and conflict precludes true freedom. It is only through intelligent choiceless awareness of one's modes of dependence that one becomes free. To ask, 'How am I to be free from dependence?' and to receive or conceive an answer to the question and proceed to do as that answer dictates, is also to create a situation of conflict. Whereas, wrote Krishnamurti,

> if you observe that a mind that depends must be confused, if you know the truth, that a mind that depends inwardly on any authority

only creates confusion – if you see that, without asking how to be free of confusion – then you will cease to depend. Then your mind becomes extraordinarily sensitive and therefore capable of learning and it disciplines itself without any form of compulsion or conformity.'[11]

Any thinking which sets up internal conflict is, according to Krishnamurti, an obstacle to freedom. He points out how much of our thinking is of this kind, for instance, comparative thinking, which is inculcated into us when we are very young. Children are told exemplary tales of heroes and saints, and urged to measure themselves up to these models. Similarly, all through our system of education, with its awarding of marks and passing and failing examinations, we are made to compare ourselves with others. This, said Krishnamurti, is really a form of aggression and violence.

> Violence is not only in killing or hitting somebody, it is in the comparative spirit. 'I must be like somebody else', or 'I must perfect myself'. Self-improvement is the very antithesis of freedom and learning. Find out for yourself how to live a life without comparing, and you will see what an extraordinary thing happens. If you really become aware, choicelessly, you will see what it means to live without comparison, never using the words 'I will be'.[11]

So ambition, which of course is a form of desire, is not the commendable and liberating thing that we are usually taught it is, for the moment we want to become something we are no longer free. 'The man who is ambitious, spiritually or otherwise, can never be without a problem, because problems cease only when the self is forgotten, when the "me" is non-existent',[2] which is of course something that cannot occur when there is comparative thinking. To revolt against the whole tradition of trying to become something, Krishnamurti said, 'is the only true revolution, leading to extraordinary freedom',[2] and to cultivate this freedom should be the real function of education. Unfortunately few educational institutions in the world perform this function which is why thinking in terms of comparison, competition and becoming remains a fundamental and rarely questioned characteristic of our minds. Only when we are free of this kind of thinking can we really begin to learn, if we understand by learning not just the acquisition of knowledge but the discovery of the new.

It is not only the confusion of the human mind, which is inherent in its habitual modes of thought, that inhibits the experience of true freedom; it is also the pettiness of the mind's habitual preoccupations and its consequent insensitivity to the whole movement and process of life in man and nature.

> The fundamental problem for the human being is the question of freedom from 'the little corner'. And that little corner is ourselves, that little corner is your shoddy little mind. We have made that little corner, because our own little minds are fragmented and therefore incapable of being sensitive to the whole; we want that little part to be made safe, peaceful, quiet, satisfying, pleasurable, thereby avoiding all pain, because, fundamentally, we are seeking pleasure.[13]

Krishnamurti's friend Aldous Huxley frequently made the point in his writings that the function of human sensory systems is to filter and limit the amount and the intensity of the experience that our minds have to deal with. Our sensory systems function to enable us to survive and work within our environment, and their sensitivity is geared to this requirement. But we know from the evidence of experiments with the effects of hypnosis and drugs that the filtering process can be temporarily suspended, whereupon it is as if the flood-gates of sensory experience of and response to the world are suddenly thrown open. Thus to expand the mind, so that it is no longer confined to 'the little corner', not fragmented and limited, but is invaded by a sense of the wholeness of life, is to be liberated from a kind of physiological bondage. Various techniques for effecting such an expansion have been explored in recent times.

Huxley advocated the controlled use of 'psychedelic' drugs like LSD, but Krishnamurti believed that there was too great a risk of dependence in such use and suggested that the same thing could be achieved by means of meditation. We shall consider his ideas and recommendations regarding meditation in a later chapter for in the present chapter we are concerned with his insights into human bondage and freedom. In this respect it is relevant to note the correspondence between Krishnamurti's ideas of the truly free mind as the mind that gets out of 'the little corner' of the self with its preoccupations with pleasure and security, and the advocacy by Huxley and others of means of expanding consciousness. We know from these reporters from 'inner space' that the experience of expanded consciousness, however it is achieved, is analogous to a mystical or religious experience, and this fact throws light on one of Krishnamurti's more elliptical definitions: that 'a mind that is free is therefore truly religious'.[11] We could say alternatively that such a mind is not bound and limited by the separatist impulses of the human mind, but is an integral part of and responsive to the whole of life.

A very illuminating formulation of Krishnamurti's is that true freedom manifests in action, not in reaction. 'Is not freedom *from* something a reaction and therefore not freedom at all?' he asked, and further:

> Is reaction away from anything freedom – or is freedom from something entirely different from reaction, standing by itself, without any motive, not dependent upon any inclination, tendency and circumstances? Is there such a thing as that kind of freedom?[9]

Of course, his contention was that there is such a thing:

> a state of mind that is so intensely active, vigorous, that it throws away every form of dependence, slavery, conformity and acceptance ... an inward state that is not dependent on any stimulus, on any knowledge.[9]

And he further maintained that only a person who is truly free in this sense is really capable of love. What we call love is generally a reaction, and our feeling love for somebody is dependent on this reaction being triggered by some physical characteristics, or combination of such characteristics, in a particular person.

Krishnamurti maintained that there is a kind of love that is not a reaction, not dependent on some particularity, but is purely an outgoing thing, a life force emanating from the inner centre of the self that does not discriminate between the objects to which it relates. For such love to come into being a person must be free, which means that he or she must be a person who acts, not one who reacts. They must have understood and transcended all the modes of human bondage and dependence, all outward and inward authority, all fear and conflict, and must furthermore have liberated their thinking and responding from the conditioning of past experience. This implies the suppression of memory and expectation. To accomplish all these things might seem to most of us to be work sufficient for a good part of a lifetime, but Krishnamurti's contention was that they could not be accomplished progressively in the course of time but only *in toto* in the present moment. The question of how this transformation might come about has only been briefly touched on in the present chapter and will be taken up in a later one. Now let us turn to the subject of Krishnamurti's philosophy of mind and consciousness.

9

On Mind, Consciousness and the Self

THE self-awareness advocated by Krishnamurti is something totally different from the self- and psychoanalysis of Freud and his followers. The process of analysis implies the existence of a self that is analysed and another self which participates in the analysis but in Krishnamurti's self-awareness there is no separation of, to use his terms, 'the observer and the observed'.

The Freudian view of human personality, with its hierarchy of the id, the ego and the superego, has profoundly influenced psychological thought in the present century, as have Freudian techniques of psychotherapy, in which 'reality testing' is employed as a means of adjusting the individual to the psychosocial norm. All this was anathema to Krishnamurti, who maintained that a personality could not realize wholeness and integrity of being from a starting point of a divisive, hierarchical view of the personality, and who regarded any kind of adjustment therapy as something which both infringes and prevents freedom. Furthermore, the method of psychoanalysis, which involves working with memories and bringing the past into the present, can only achieve a stabilization of the self according to a pattern laid down by past experience. If it manages to achieve such a stabilization, it strengthens the false idea that the self is a permanent entity which develops individuality in the course of time through the exercise of the faculties of will, understanding and intelligence.

A practising psychologist and analyst once told Krishnamurti how a woman, whom he had been treating for several months for severe depressions, without success, had gained a sense of release, and ultimately a cure, from attending a series of Krishnamurti's talks. He asked if Krishnamurti could recommend a method or technique which would not require the amount of time and patient investigation demanded by psychoanalysis, but would alleviate human miseries and depressions quickly. Krishnamurti did not answer the question directly, but asked the psychoanalyst what he tried to do with his patients. He replied that he tried to help them overcome their difficulties and depressions so that they could fit into society. To the question whether it was important to help people fit into a corrupt society, the analyst answered that it was not his function to reform society or to try to create supernormal people. But, Krishnamurti persisted, 'if one is only concerned with helping the individual to conform to the existing social pattern . . . is one not maintaining the very causes that make for frustration, misery and destruction?'[4] Psychoanalysis, apparently, was not concerned with the total development of man, but only with a part of his consciousness. It was surely obvious that to attempt to treat a part, without having an understanding of the whole that it was part of, could actually cause other kinds of trouble or disease. The analyst admitted that there was something in this argument, and that his profession tended to be too specialized and narrow in its view of man. However, he asked again whether Krishnamurti could recommend a method or technique of therapy, not realizing that the very question implied the narrow and superficial view of man which he had just admitted to be wrong. 'Can a method or technique set man free?' Krishnamurti asked, 'or will it merely shape him to a desired end?' No reply from the analyst is on record, but the discussion up to this point clearly brought out the difference between Krishnamurti's psychological ideas and those of a modern orthodox psychologist.

Over the last hundred years or so, psychological thought has made much of the distinction between the conscious and the unconscious or subconscious mind. There has been a strong bias, largely through the influence of Freud, to regard the unconscious as a realm of chaos which gives rise to destructive and disruptive passions that need to be brought under the control of the rational consciousness. Psychologists speak of the 'threshold' of consciousness, proposing that all that is above this threshold is accessible to introspection, and all that is below it is not so accessible but requires some special technique, such as dream interpretation, to make it so.

Krishnamurti made use of the distinction between the conscious and the unconscious, but without the bias and the dichotomous tendency of the orthodox Freudian view. He preferred to speak of the different layers or levels of the mind, and he asked:

> Is the conscious mind different from the unconscious mind? We have divided the conscious from the unconscious; is this justified? Is this true? Is there such a division . . . a definite barrier, a line where the conscious ends and the unconscious begins?[2]

To say that we are aware of our unconscious does not make sense, and as the unconscious is not a datum of our experience the term is really only an aid to our thinking and talking about the mind: the division between the two aspects of mind is a projection out of our inherent confusion, a reflection of our divisive habits of thought.

If we speak of the levels of the mind, one thing we can observe is that the upper levels have been educated, trained, disciplined, conditioned according to the dictates of our reason, which is itself dictated to by society, culture and what we conceive of as our needs. 'Is the unconscious, the deeper level, uneducated?' Krishnamurti asked. He answered the question in the affirmative, but did not deplore the fact and call for the extension of rational understanding and control to the deeper layers, on the contrary he regarded it as a good thing that these layers should remain uneducated, for:

> In the deeper layers there may be the source and means of finding out new things, because the superficial layers have become mechanical, they are conditioned; repetitive, imitative; there is no freedom to find out, to move, to fly, to take to the wind! And in the deeper layers, which are not educated, which are unsophisticated and therefore extraordinarily primitive – primitive, not savage – there may be the source of something new.[11]

This affirmation of the unconscious and its processes, of the validity and use of the deeper levels of the mind, is one of the positive aspects of Krishnamurti's teaching. If we do not set up a purely theoretical barrier or threshold between the conscious and unconscious, he implies, we can encourage, instead of inhibiting, the flow of communication between the different levels of the mind, and thus be more whole and spontaneous in our moment-to-moment living. We will thereby become truly creative. Analytical processes cannot be creative in the deepest sense of the word because creativity is an impulse of the whole being. Analysis involves fragmentation, which means one fragment of the whole assumes authority over the other parts as well as assuming the objectivity to examine them critically. 'Any exaggeration of any fragment of the whole consciousness,' wrote Krishnamurti, 'any emphasis on any fragment, is a form of neurosis',[11] and exaggeration of the intellectual, analytical functions of the mind is as much a form of neurosis as exaggeration of emotional or spiritual aspects.

Human beings need a sense of individual personal identity, and sometimes they obtain this by identifying themselves with one of the fragments of their total personality. Then sometimes they may realize that such an identification is neurotic, or become dissatisfied with the narrowness and limitations of it. They seek to redress the balance by identifying themselves with as many other fragments as possible in the hope of achieving wholeness, of integrating all the fragments. But if we stop to ask the question, 'Who is this entity trying to identify itself with the other fragments?' we see immediately that it is impossible to realize wholeness in this way. The very idea that there is a separate self that can be identified with different fragments is dualistic to start with, and that basic dualism is never resolved by the process of identification.

'There is only one state,' Krishnamurti asserted, 'not two states such as the conscious and the unconscious; there is only a state of being, which is consciousness.'[2] So the next question is, what is consciousness? Is it something independent of its content, or is it entirely defined by and made up of its content?

> If consciousness is made up of my despair, my anxiety, fears, pleasures, the innumerable hopes, guilts and the vast experience of the past, then any action springing from that consciousness can never free the consciousness from its limitations...[11]

Krishnamurti proposed that the investigation of the question whether consciousness can ever empty itself of its content and be free is of supreme importance 'if there is to be a radical change in the human mind, and therefore in society'.[11]

If we attend to the functions of the mind, we will realize that consciousness is always of the past. We are conscious only of things that are over. The psychologist William James coined the term 'the stream of consciousness', and the metaphor may be employed to elucidate Krishnamurti's thinking on the subject. Consciousness is a movement, a flow, of mental events, and that flow is always from past to future: at any moment the content of consciousness is so identified with this flow, so determined by the past and the future, by memories and expectations, that the present is excluded from it.

Krishnamurti used the analogy of a pendulum, proposing that

the normal state of consciousness is a swinging backwards and forwards between the past and the future, which is a movement that excludes anything new because the future comes into being as a projection of the past and, although it may become slightly modified by the movement, it is really the past in another guise. Consciousness that is bound up in this movement is incapable of seeing a fact simply as a fact, and the question is whether consciousness can ever be something other than this movement which excludes the present. In the constant swinging of a pendulum there is an infinitesimal interval of complete stillness each time the pendulum reaches the extremity of its swing, and Krishnamurti suggested that the analogy applied in this respect too, in that in consciousness there are intervals between thoughts.

> Between two thoughts there is a period of silence which is not related to the thought process. If you observe you will see that that period of silence, that interval, is not of time, and the discovery of that interval, the full experiencing of that interval, liberates you from conditioning.[2]

To become focused upon these intervals, he further proposed, is the meaning of meditation.

By way of illustration of his argument, Krishnamurti sometimes asked his audience whether a person who exclaims, 'How happy I am!' really is happy. 'The moment you are conscious you are happy, is happiness there?' he asked. He argued that it is not, that the happiness we become conscious of is already past, and that the formulation of the thought, 'How happy I am!' is an instance of the swing from the past into a future determined by that past, in which the present is annulled. This implies that when we really are happy, the very experience of that happiness is such that there is no room for consciousness of it, which seems to mean that Krishnamurti set little value upon consciousness and was advocating the cultivation of a state of mind that is somehow exclusive of, or prior to, consciousness. On the other hand, many of the people who are interested in his teaching are those who also commonly speak of the heightening or expanding of consciousness as an ideal, and it is relevant to inquire how Krishnamurti's apparent disavowal of the importance of consciousness can be reconciled with this kind of idealism.

Well, it can be reconciled, because what Krishnamurti was advocating was not the cultivation of an unconscious state. but of what he called 'the silent mind'. This comes into being when the mind empties itself of its content, of the known, and is not a state of mindlessness but a state of intense and clear awareness of 'what is'. This awareness is not a movement of the mind. Movement is characteristic of the conscious mind, but the silent mind is free of movement, although it is fully aware of the movements of consciousness. The silent mind can be aware of the stream of thoughts that flow through the conscious mind, but it does not discriminate between them in terms of value, importance or rightness; it just observes the flow. This observation without judgement, this passive awareness or 'choiceless awareness' of the flowing stream of consciousness is by no means a negative thing. In fact it can be very positive and effective in dealing with problems of any kind. It has the effect of breaking down the barriers between the different levels of consciousness, thus facilitating the flow between the unconscious and the conscious levels. As a result of this, psychological problems tend just to go away, to become non-problems, and even practical or intellectual problems may yield a solution because the intuitive and creative faculties of the unconscious are given full and free play.

Krishnamurti's epistemology, then, consists in the postulation and investigation of a non-conceptual and non-dualistic mode of knowing, and in the assertion that it is only by means of this mode that we can know reality. Closely tied in with his thinking on this subject is his philosophy of the self.

The young Krishnamurti, as we have seen, had certain experiences, which he described as union with 'the Beloved', clearly involving a sense of liberation from his individual consciousness and a merging with or participating in a higher and quite impersonal consciousness. So real and all-important were these experiences to him that he could make such statements as: 'If you would understand, you must look through my mind. If you would feel, you must look through my heart',[1] with the implication that his mind and heart did not have the qualities of partiality, particularity and limitation that characterized other people's, but in some way participated in and were means of access to universality, and thus in a sense not really *his* at all. At this stage of his life, Krishnamurti had difficulty elucidating his basic experiences and ideas. He would sometimes speak of liberation as the disappearance of the 'I' and at other times say that it consisted in the fulfilment or consummation of the 'I'. He would urge people to 'realise themselves and become great', or to 'die to the self'. But the verbal difficulties he had do not invalidate the significance of the experience that he was trying to describe. That experience which could equally truly, if not very helpfully, be described as the death of the self or the consummation of the self, remained a focal point of his later thinking.

Krishnamurti asks us to consider what the sense of the self consists of and how it arises. In early infancy a human being does not have any concept of the self; the first distinctions he makes between the self and the not-self relate only to the body. But the process that begins with distinguishing 'my hand' and 'my foot' extends by degrees to identifying a whole complex of feelings, experiences, thoughts, ideas, impulses, desires, memories, hopes, fears, and so on, as 'mine'; this complex constitutes the self. When we examine these components of the self, however, we may suffer a blow to our pride, because they are all derived from our environment and culture. The entire complex only comprises an individuality in the sense that the number of components and the ways in which they combine and interact is unique, which is not really a kind of individuality commensurate with the degree of self-esteem and sense of self-importance that most people have. This self, in fact, is just a bundle of perceptions and memories, but the more actions we perform, imagining that it is the self that originates and executes them, the more substance we endow to this really insubstantial entity, and the more we come under the thralldom of the past. As it gains substance, the self assumes authority, takes it upon itself to mediate between consciousness and reality, or rather intrudes itself continually between the mind and 'what is', so that it becomes a positive impediment to knowing.

Now if you say that the self is an illusion or a delusion, many people will protest, feeling that their very identity and existence are somehow threatened. But very likely many of these same people will admit to a sense of dissatisfaction with the self, a feeling that it is too limited, too undeveloped, and will be looking for kinds of experiences that 'take them out of themselves' or constitute an experience of 'self-transcendence'. This ambivalent attitude to the self, this simultaneous clinging to it and wanting to be free of it, is very common, but for most of us the self has taken on such substance and reality that the proposition of its non-existence seems preposterous. Even to seek and aspire to be free of it seems an absurdity, for we wonder who is doing the seeking and aspiring if not the self.

'Can the "I" positively set about abnegating itself?' Krishnamurti asked, and he proceeded to show that the task is impossible:

> If it does, its motive, its intention, is to gain that which is not to be possessed. Whatever its activity, however noble its aim, any effort on the part of the 'I' is still within the field of its own memories, idiosyncracies and projections, whether conscious or unconscious. The 'I' may divide itself into the organic 'I' and the 'non-I' or transcendental self; but this dualistic separation is an illusion in which the mind is caught. Whatever may be the movement of the mind of the 'I', it can never free itself; it may go from level to level, from stupid to more intelligent choice, but its movement will always be within the sphere of its own making.[4]

So it appears that we are in a trap, that because of the intrusion of the self we are cut off from the new, from reality, and condemned to a future which is but a projection of the past. Is there no way out of this situation? Krishnamurti maintained that there is: through awareness, attention, through practising the non-dualistic mode of knowing, we can become self-less. And this means not only getting into a more authentic relationship with 'what is', removing the screen between consciousness and reality, but also overcoming such tribulations of the human condition as fear, pain and suffering, for these exist only as experiences of the self.

This last point needs to be elucidated, because it is a central teaching of Krishnamurti's, and one in which he re-states, in his own way, the traditional Buddhist teaching on the overcoming of sorrow, fear and suffering. All our troubles, he said, arise from our dualistic way of thinking, which makes us imagine that experiences are something we *have* rather than something we *are*, that there are two distinct entities, the experiencer and the experience, the observer and the observed.

> When there is no *observer* who is suffering, is the suffering different from you? You *are* the suffering, are you not? You are not apart from the pain, you *are* the pain. What happens? There is no labelling, there is no giving it a name and thereby brushing it aside – you are merely that pain, that feeling, that sense of agony. When you are that, what happens? Do you say you suffer then? Surely, a fundamental transformation has taken place. Then there is no longer 'I suffer', because there is no centre to suffer, and the centre suffers because we have never examined what it is.[2]

Krishnamurti often used the term 'the centre' as synonymous with the self, and the term lends itself to an illuminating illustration of his ideas. A centre has space outside it, and that space is limited by the centre, it has a circumference determined by the centre. There is this centre, which has its own dimensions, borders within which it recognizes the 'me', and outside it there is a space, and although the centre may be able to expand this space – for instance by taking psychoactive drugs – it cannot expand it very significantly but must always remain trapped within the limitations of its own making. As Krishnamurti vividly put it:

> The little monkey may meditate, may follow many systems, but that monkey will always remain; and therefore the space it will create for itself will always be limited and shallow.[11]

Most of our actions issue from the centre, and all our feelings and perceptions are qualified by the centre so long as we regard them as things we *have*. But there are times when suddenly we find that we are looking, living or feeling without a centre, although these times are usually of short duration. This is because thought seizes upon the experience, dwells on it or wants to continue it, and this thought, which is the past trying to project itself into the future, becomes the new centre. We can, however, by practising passive choiceless awareness, begin to look, live and feel without the centre for longer periods, without the noisy, opinionated and demanding self intruding and spoiling the experience. This annulling of the centre, this death of the self, is not the awful end of everything that we might have feared when we first contemplated the prospect, because *life* goes on.

> Life goes on, but without the 'me' as the observer. Life goes on, the registration goes on, memory goes on, but the 'me' which thought has brought about, which is the content of consciousness, that 'me' disappears: obviously because that 'me' is limited. Therefore thought as the 'me' says 'I am limited'. It does not mean that the body does not go on, but the centre, which is the activity as the self, as the 'me', is not. Again that is logical because thought says 'I am limited. I will not create the "me" which is further limitation.' It realises it and it drops away.[15]

Descriptions such as this, of the non-dualistic and non-conceptual ways of knowing and living, abound in Krishnamurti's talks and writings. They are all means of trying to convey the nature and meaning of experiences which he personally underwent. When we recall his descriptions of these experiences, and the quite considerable pain and suffering he went through, even as late as 1961, in the period covered by the *Notebook*, we are prompted to wonder whether the switch-over to the alternative mode of knowing, and the dissolution of the self as centre, necessitates or involves some actual physical change in the body. Krishnamurti believed that it does, that in some way the brain and its processes change, that even the neuronal firing of the brain cells ceases and established circuits of brain activity, of stimulus-response patterns, are wiped out. 'Can there be a mutation in the brain?' he asked, and answered: 'We say it is possible . . . when there is a great shock of attention.'[17]

Whether this is what actually occurred when he himself underwent 'the process' must be a matter of conjecture, but we do know from recent researches in the area of electronic monitoring of brain activity that non-ordinary mental states, for instance of the meditator or healer, have corresponding distinct brain states. The philosophical question whether mind and brain are distinct entities is not resolved by these observations, however, nor did Krishnamurti go into it, though he did say that 'thought is a material process, a chemical process'.[17] This could be taken as a statement favouring what is known as the identity theory, according to which every mind-event or -state has its corresponding brain-event or -state, therefore there is no component of human personality antecedent to the development of the individual brain or that survives its death. This is a theory which, for obvious reasons, religious people find intolerable, so most religions incline to a dualistic view of man, as composed of a physical brain and a non-physical mind. As we have seen, however, Krishnamurti considered dualistic thinking as a block to the perception of truth, and the concept of 'wholeness' is central to his thinking. Indeed he does sometimes seem to be speaking as a materialist, from what is known as a monist position, particularly in regarding thought and consciousness in terms of brain-cell activity. On the other hand, he speaks of the silent mind generating no brain activity, although it is intensely aware and in touch with reality. So to assign him to the materialist camp, as some critics have done, is to act on a partial and superficial understanding of his thought. Needless to say, Krishnamurti himself, who regarded naming and labelling as pursuits of the dull mind, was indifferent to which camp he might be assigned to.

While we are on the subject of Krishnamurti's philosophy of mind, let us be clear about what he meant by two terms which he frequently used with rather special significance: memory and intelligence.

We have seen that he tended to regard memory as a primary

cause of human bondage because it continually makes the future conform to the pattern of the past and thus prevents experience or perception of the new. But to understand this proposition clearly we have to distinguish between factual memory and psychological memory. My memory of any event may contain both components: the memory of precisely what happened and the memory of the feelings or reactions I had with regard to the happening. When Krishnamurti said that the mind should be clear of its burden of memories he was not suggesting that factual memories should be expunged. Obviously our factual memories enable us to live and conduct ourselves in the world with as much efficiency as we do. Although a person without them might have the joy of encountering the new at every moment, his moments would be few indeed unless he had somebody to look after him all the time. So we need our factual memories for practical purposes, but the trouble is that the human mind does not clearly distinguish between factual and psychological memories. We tend to carry with us a large complement of the latter type, and it is with this battery of psychological memories that we meet life, meet every new situation and challenge, with the result that we always assimilate the new to the old and so never experience the novelty of it. When Krishnamurti advocated the clearing out of memories from the mind, it was these psychological memories, of past thoughts, feelings and reactions, to which he was referring.

A mind thus cleared becomes intelligent in Krishnamurti's sense of the term. To be intelligent has nothing to do with being knowledgeable. In fact:

> When you say 'I know', you are on the path of non-intelligence; but when you say 'I don't know', and really mean it, you have already started on the path of intelligence. When a man doesn't know, he looks, listens, inquires. 'To know' is to accumulate, and he who accumulates will never know: he is not intelligent.[5]

Nor has intelligence to do with intellectual or any other capacity.

> Capacity is not intelligence. Intelligence is sensitive awareness of the totality of life; life with its problems, contradictions, miseries, joys. To be aware of all this, without choice and without being caught up in any one of its issues and to flow with the whole of life is intelligence.[16]

True intelligence, then, consists in looking, listening, inquiring and being choicelessly aware. It is a function of the mind that is simple, in the sense that it is uncluttered with convictions, opinions, habits of thinking in terms of measurement or comparison. It is not personal, and it is quite different from thought.

> You may be very clever, very good at arguing, very learned. You may have experienced, lived a tremendous life, been all over the world, investigating, searching, looking, accumulating a great deal of knowledge, practised Zen or Hindu meditation. But all that has nothing to do with intelligence. Intelligence comes into being when the mind, the heart and the body are really harmonious.[13]

As intelligence comes of harmony, actions governed by it bring harmony into the world. Morality and virtue, then, are not the observance of prescriptions or principles, but consist in the spontaneous functioning of intelligence in the world, which 'naturally brings about order and the beauty of order'. This, Krishnamurti maintained, 'is a religious life'.[13]

Which brings us to another major topic.

10

On Religion and the Religious Life

ALTHOUGH Krishnamurti disparaged all thought born of reaction or of past experience, it is difficult to conceive that his own thinking on the subject of religion was not profoundly influenced by reaction to his Theosophical upbringing, and by his early experience of being regarded by thousands as the new Messiah, the vehicle of the Lord Maitreya. As we have seen, in the ecstatic experiences he had as a young man, he was quite convinced that he separated from his physical body and went into the presence of the Master Kuthumi and the Lord Maitreya, actually discoursing with them and bringing back pearls of wisdom from their lips. Reflecting on this years later, he acknowledged the vividness of the experience at the time, and the conviction it had carried, but put it down to his suggestibility and the influence of the Theosophists, particularly Leadbeater. In his mature philosophy, Krishnamurti left open the question of the existence of a supermundane world or dimension and of superphysical beings, concerning himself with the psychology of religious belief and experience, and investigating the nature of religion and the religious life.

Krishnamurti was fond of telling the story about God and the Devil seeing man chance upon and pick up a shining object, which turns out to be truth. God is delighted and remarks that the Devil is going to have a tough time now, but the Devil is unperturbed and says, 'Not at all; I am going to help him organize it.' In Krishnamurti's view, the human mind's organizing tendency, which is a function of thought, is unconditionally an obstacle and impediment to the search for truth. No subject elicited his contempt – and he could on occasion by scathingly contemptuous – as surely as did that of organized religion and its devotees. He observed with unarguable logic that man has been what he calls religious for thousands of years but is still bellicose, murderous, confused and petty. Religions, he conceded, have had some civilizing influence, but this is greatly outweighed by the mischief they have wrought in the world, by the cruelty and tyranny that man has imposed on man in their name, and by the falsehoods and cynical deceptions, masquerading as divine truths and mysteries, that they have foisted on people for the sake of maintaining priestly power and privilege.

He did not take the liberal attitude that a man's religion should be respected and that one of the fundamental freedoms is the freedom to worship. He was quite uncompromising – some would say uncharitable and destructive – when people protested, as some did, that he was destroying their religion without putting anything in its place. He replied: 'What is false must be put away if what is true is to be.'[5] He remained unmoved when people told him that through religion they had found comfort, understanding and love. When a palpably good man described to him his devotional life and the joy he had in it, saying, 'I spend my days in the shadow of God', Krishnamurti was unimpressed and asked, 'Isn't it important to find out if the shadow has any substance behind it?'[4] In such encounters, his simplicity and his logic cut through all forms of piety and complacency and were devastating.

The propositions that people must believe in something, and that a person without belief is somehow incapacitated for confronting life's problems and opportunities, would probably have the assent of the majority, but in Krishnamurti's view they are dangerous clichés because they endorse a species of mental idleness that is crippling. He wrote:

> Belief is one thing, reality is another . . . One leads to bondage and the other is possible only in freedom . . . Belief can never lead to reality. Belief is the result of conditioning, or the outcome of fear, or the result of an outer or inner authority which gives comfort. Reality is none of these . . . The credulous are always willing to believe, accept, obey, whether what is offered is good or bad, mischievous or beneficial. The believing mind is not an enquiring mind, so it remains within the limits of the formula or principle.[8]

There is a specious argument, often used by religious proselytizers and apologists, which for Christians particularly carries the weight of scriptural authority, which is that belief is a prerequisite of the revelation of the truth that is believed. 'Only believe and you will see', they urge, and, echoing the Jesus of the Gospels, they harangue sceptics as 'Ye of little faith'. The story of the disciple 'doubting Thomas' is told in such a way as to elicit contempt for his reluctance to believe in what was by any standards a pretty incredible event. On a more sophisticated level there were theologians like Tertullian who argued that the Christian story was believable precisely because it was so impossible and absurd ('*credo quia absurdum est*'), and philosophers like Kierkegaard who advocated a 'leap' into faith when reason and logic proved incapable of ascertaining the truths of religion. So at all levels in Christian cultures this rather extraordinary proposition, that you will never know what to believe in unless you believe in it before you know it, has been promulgated. Reasonable people, quite ready to concede that their mental endowment for apprehending the truth is fallible, have been persuaded by it to relinquish inquiry in favour of faith, hoping to reap a reward for their acquiescence, at the very least in an afterlife and, they hope, in this life, in the form of a marvellously fulfilling or revelatory spiritual experience.

Krishnamurti had no time for such casuistry, and by shifting the argument from the philosophical plane to the psychological he showed it up for the tendentious sophistry that it is:

> Through experience you hope to touch the truth of your belief, to prove it to yourself, but this belief conditions your experience. It isn't that the experience comes to prove the belief, but rather that the belief begets the experience. Your belief in God will give you the experience of what you call God. You will always experience what you believe and nothing else. And this invalidates your experience. The Christian will see virgins, angels and Christ, the Hindu will see similar deities in extravagant plurality. The Muslim, the Buddhist, the Jew and the Communist are all the same. Belief conditions its own supposed proof.[10]

Krishnamurti knew from experience what he was talking about. Had he not seen and conversed with the Master Kuthumi and the Lord Maitreya when he had believed in them? The experience had been intoxicating and utterly convincing at the time, but it had not given him any grasp of ultimate truth. In fact it was only when he ceased to believe that he began to see things clearly. 'When the mind is free of belief, then it can look,'[10] he later said, implying of course that really being able to look at 'what is' is the beginning of wisdom.

Another pious injunction open to the same criticism as the

advocacy of belief is the encouragement of the spiritual quest in the terms, 'Seek and thou shall find'. Naturally, Krishnamurti said, the human mind always finds what it seeks; that is the trouble. Thought projects its own hopes, fears and longings, shuts its eyes and counts up to a hundred, then trots off in search of them; finding them is no hard task because they never stray far from their origin and they want to be found anyway. That is the religious quest, but it is not the quest for truth, which is a quest that demands no preconceptions, no influence from hopes, fears and longings, and the total commitment of the free intelligence of an awakened and aware mind.

Again adopting the psychological point of view, Krishnamurti regarded the religious quest, and the sanctification of it in legend and literature, as inspired by man's sense of mortality and existential loneliness, also by the fear and confusion that this engenders. He wrote:

> Man has always been seeking something beyond his own death, beyond his own problems, something that will be enduring, true and timeless. He has called it God, he has given it many names; and most of us believe in something of this kind, without ever actually experiencing it.[13]

But to embark upon a search for this 'something beyond', Krishnamurti argued, is an illogical quixotic enterprise, because if man did not know from experience what he was looking for he would not recognize it even if he found it, and if he did have experience of it he would not need to search.

Such an argument will seem to the religious to be as sophistical as the 'only believe...' argument appeared to Krishnamurti, and no pilgrim of eternity is going to be turned back by what he may regard as a logical cavil. But when Krishnamurti became mischievous or scornful in argument, it was generally because he saw frivolity and superficiality in matters that demand commitment and seriousness. 'When you are enquiring into such an extraordinary question', he told an audience in New York in 1971,

> there must be the freedom of actually not knowing a thing about it. You really don't know, do you? You don't know what truth is, what God is – if there is such a thing – or what is a truly religious mind. You have read about it, people have talked about it for millennia, have built monasteries, but actually they are living on other people's knowledge, experience and propaganda. To find out, surely one must put aside all that completely, and therefore the enquiry into all this is a

very serious matter. If you want to play with it, there are all kinds of so called spiritual, religious entertainments, but they have no value whatsoever to a serious mind.[13]

The Romantic attitude to man's religious aspirations sees in his 'divine discontent', his 'immortal longings', his persistent feeling that there must be something more to life and the universe than he has experienced, a kind of noble restlessness that drives him, like Goethe's *ewige weibliche*, 'ever onward and upward'. Krishnamurti took a cool view of this attitude, remarking that 'in the demand for something more lies deception', and that 'deception is easy if one craves for some kind of experience'.[13] He asked how that craving arises, and suggested that it is because we get bored with our ordinary everyday experiences. 'Do people who aspire to a transcendental experience wonder whether such a thing exists?' he asked. Again, 'How would they know if they had one, lacking prior experience?' The aspiration itself, whatever the poets and ecstatics may say, is, Krishnamurti maintained, '*essentially* wrong', and in support of his contention he argued that the genuinely free person does not have it.

> I find that as long as the mind is in a state of fear, it wants to escape from it, and it projects the idea of the Supreme, and wants to experience that. But if it frees itself from its own agony then it is altogether in a different state. It doesn't even ask for the experience because it is at a different level.[13]

Devotion and worship are almost universally lauded practices, but like most other aspects of conventional religion they drew Krishnamurti's scorn. 'In ourselves we are so petty', he wrote,

> so essentially nothing, and the worship of something greater than ourselves is as petty and stupid as we are. Identification with the great is still a projection of the small. The more is an extension of the less. The small in search of the large will only find what it is capable of finding.[4]

The devotee who protests his love of the object of his devotion, and falls back on the argument that expressing such love gives him deep satisfaction and does no harm to others, would not get any concession or comfort from Krishnamurti, but only a barrage of rhetorical questions with implied negative answers:

> Is it selflessness to lose yourself in a book, in a chant, in an idea? Is devotion the worship of an image, of a person, of a symbol? Can a

symbol ever represent truth? Is not a symbol static, and can a static thing ever represent that which is living?[4]

If these questions are not enough to discomfit the worshipper, there is an even more fundamental and devastating argument: that the worshipper is also the worshipped. The early Greek philosopher Euhemeros made the same point when he said that if a horse could conceive of God he would conceive of Him in the shape of a horse. Krishnamurti maintained that the object of worship, however abstractly it may be symbolized, must be a creation of thought, a projection of a person's hopes, fears, and so on, as conditioned by his background.

> Your image is your intoxicant, and it is carved out of your own memory; you are worshipping yourself through the image created by your own thought. Your devotion is the love of yourself covered over by the chant of your mind.[4]

When Mahatma Gandhi, in India in the 1930s, was speaking out against the tradition that only Brahmins could enter temples, Krishnamurti travelled around with him for some time and on one occasion was asked what he thought about this teaching. His answer was even more scandalous in the eyes of the faithful than Gandhi's proposal that anyone should be allowed in the temples. He said, 'God is not in temples, so it doesn't matter who enters.'[17]

When the question arose, 'Is nothing, then, sacred?' Krishnamurti recommended the questioner to try an experiment. Take a stick or a piece of stone, he said, put it on your mantelpiece and every day place a fresh flower in front of it, at the same time saying something like 'Om', or 'Amen'. Do this for a month, and you will see how holy that stick or stone has become, although of course only your devotion has made it so; it is not really different from any other you might pick up by the roadside. So the answer to the question is that nothing that is created by thought is sacred.

Krishnamurti's polemic was not against man's need for experience of the sacred, but against the stratagems he unconsciously employs to fulfil that need, and the unworthy objects that he cravenly allows to gratify it.

> Unless human beings find sacredness their life really has no meaning, it is an empty shell. They may be very orderly, they may be relatively free, but unless there is this thing that is totally sacred, untouched by thought, life has no deep meaning.[17]

And he put the fundamental question:

> Is there something sacred, or is everything matter, everything thought, everything transient, everything impermanent? Is there something that thought can never touch and therefore is incorruptible, timeless, eternal and sacred?[17]

In his own experience there was, but its existence and nature, he said, are difficult to convey in words, which are the creation and the vehicle of thought, and thought has to cease before the sacred becomes manifest. Perhaps the most that can be said is: 'That which *is*, is sacred.'[13]

In his *Notebook*, that illuminating record of his inner life and experiences over a period of several months, Krishnamurti made a strong assertion of the existence of the sacred, although what he had to say about it would afford little sustenance for the God-hungry:

> There's a sacredness which is not of thought, nor of a feeling resuscitated by thought. It is not recognisable by thought nor can it be utilised by thought. Thought cannot formulate it. But there's a sacredness, untouched by any symbol or word. It is not communicable. It is a fact.
>
> A fact is to be seen and the seeing is not through the word. When a fact is interpreted it ceases to be a fact; it becomes something entirely different. The seeing is of the highest importance. The seeing is out of time-space; it's immediate, instantaneous. And what's seen is never the same again.
>
> This sacredness has no worshipper, the observer who meditates upon it. It's not in the market to be bought or sold. Like beauty, it cannot be seen through its opposite for it has no opposite.[16]

Here we come to the positive aspect of Krishnamurti's philosophy of religion, after his devastating critique of its conventional forms and concepts. For all his strictures against believers, worshippers, ecstatics and enthusiasts, Krishnamurti himself was clearly a modern mainstream figure in the venerable Indian tradition of the holy man and teacher. No matter that he repudiated any following as well as the role of guru, adopting Western modes of casual dress and occasional vernacular turns of speech, he was nevertheless what all but the most bigoted sectarian would regard as a religious man. So let us now see what he had to say on the positive side about religion and the religious life.

'We mean by religion', he wrote, 'the gathering together of all energy to investigate . . . if there is anything sacred.'[17] And again:

> One has to investigate without any motive, without any purpose, the facts of time and if there is a timeless state. To enquire into that means to have no belief whatsoever, not to be committed to any religion, to any so-called spiritual organisation, not to follow any guru, and therefore to have no authority whatsoever.[13]

Being religious, then, implies dedication if not devotion, an intense dedication to investigating what is truth. Put aphoristically: 'The search for truth is true religion, and the man who is seeking truth is the only religious man.'[6] It may be objected that according to this definition there is no difference between the religious man and the philosopher, until we recall that the investigation into what is truth is not an intellectual exercise, a function of thought, but cannot begin until thought has ceased, until the self has been negated, and consciousness has been emptied of the impedimenta of memory, habit and conditioning. This work prior to investigation is more in the line of what is commonly acknowledged to be part of the religious life, for it involves total commitment, the recognition of an unregenerate state of being, and the exercise of certain faculties with a view to transcending that state.

But what are these faculties? The question again takes us away from what is conventionally regarded as the religious life. The regimens and disciplines of monks, who seek through them to coerce a recalcitrant and continually backsliding mind and body into the paths of godliness, were not advocated by Krishnamurti. 'Is the denial of pleasure or beauty a way that leads to a religious life?' he asked. 'Can a tortured, twisted, distorted mind ever find what is a religious life?'[10] No, the very nature of discipline is the setting up of an inner conflict, the pitting of one set of desires against another. As all desires are the creation of the self and of thought, such conflict is the very antithesis of the religious life.

On one of his visits to India, Krishnamurti was visited by a man who had lived a rigorously ascetic life for thirty years, denying his body any kind of comfort, suppressing all desires, meditating long hours and fasting for days at a time. Despite all these disciplines, however, he found himself in a state of frustration. He said that it was as if he had come up against a wall which would not be broken down; his mind could not reach beyond a certain point, yet he felt that there must be a stage beyond and that to reach it was the whole purpose of the ascetic life. He said he had talked to many other ascetics who had had the same experience of disappointment and frustration. Some believed that the breakthrough would eventually come with more arduous self-discipline and denial, but this man felt that he would never get any further.

He was right, Krishnamurti said, no amount of effort could break down the wall. But perhaps he should consider a different approach to his problem. At present a part of his mind was trying to capture and dominate the whole, and even if it succeeded, that would not create a harmonious wholeness. He should ask himself whether it was not possible to approach the problems of life totally, with the whole of his being.

The ascetic confessed that he didn't really understand what Krishnamurti meant, and he wanted some direction as to what he should do. Krishnamurti said that he should not be concerned with doing anything, but only with discovering the feeling of the whole of his being, because 'this feeling has its own action'. Right action would follow naturally when there was feeling without withholding, thinking undistorted by fear, and no seeking of a specific result. 'But', said the ascetic, 'must not our desires be tamed?' Krishnamurti answered that to find truth required tremendous energy, and the deliberate suppression of desire produced inner conflict which dissipated this essential energy. So how, asked the ascetic, can one conserve energy? 'The desire to conserve energy is greed,' he was told. 'This essential energy cannot be conserved or accumulated; it comes into being with the cessation of contradiction within oneself.' But should that not be attained, asked the ascetic, by the type of meditation he had been practising for years, by making the mind one-pointed? No, Krishnamurti said,

> such intensity is a hindrance to reality, because it is the result of limiting, narrowing down the mind through the action of will; and will is desire. There is an intensity which is wholly different: the strange intensity that comes with total being, that is, when one's whole being is integrated, not put together through the desire for a result.[4]

The wall that the ascetic felt that he was up against was really his ego; it was the self, and all efforts of the self to break through its own barriers only served to strengthen those barriers. The understanding of the truth of this was the thing required to initiate a movement of the whole. The ascetic was grateful for the insight he had been given, and said in conclusion, 'My life has been an incessant struggle, but now I see the possibility of ending this conflict.'[4]

This discussion is typical of many in which Krishnamurti expressed his conviction that to be religious means to think, feel and act out of the totality of one's being, which means out of a quiet mind, 'because only such a mind is a religious mind, sees the whole of life as a unit, a unitary movement . . . [and] acts totally, not fragmentarily'.[13] Such a conception of the religious life rules out any distinction between it and the worldly life: a distinction which is made in most religions, but is a creation of thought with its divisive habits. In point of fact, anyone who considers himself to be religious or spiritual exhibits a mentality which is the very essence of worldliness. The same goes for anybody who disparages the material in favour of some idea of the spiritual, if only for the very practical reason that 'without the world of matter, the material world, we wouldn't be here'.[13] There is great beauty in the material world, and the enjoyment of it, through really seeing 'what is', is an integral part of the religious life, as is the understanding that to make of this enjoyment a centre, a focus of thought, is the surest way to kill it, arousing those qualities that in many theologies are characterized as demons, for instance lust, greed, envy and despair.

In Buddhism and Christianity the quality which above all distinguishes the religious man is compassion, or love. It was for Krishnamurti, too, but he did not regard this love as something that could be elicited by teaching, by precept, or by any kind of deliberation, for it consists in a spontaneous and unmotivated movement of consciousness towards the object. 'To be religious is to be sensitive to reality,' he wrote, and 'from this sensitivity to the whole of existence springs goodness, love'.[6] And again:

> You can only find out what love is by knowing what it is not. Not knowing intellectually, but actually in life putting aside what it is not – jealousy, ambition and greed, all division that goes on in life, the me and the you, we and they, black and white . . .[6]

Religion, then, is incompatible with piety, with religiosity, with institutions and the institutionalizing mind; it is a way of being in the world, of seeing and relating to the world and its phenomena. It is not a yearning after the superhuman or the supermundane, but on the contrary is a realization of full humanness and of the sacredness of the mundane world, of 'what is'. The religious mind is quiet, detached, non-seeking, non-believing, highly sensitive and creative. It is orderly and virtuous, and when it governs action it creates order and virtue, not in observance of moral fiats and prohibitions but because the action is an impulse within a harmonious and self-regulating totality.

All religions teach how to attain to the state that they represent as ideal, but Krishnamurti is original – some might say perverse – in insisting that to ask how is to automatically disqualify oneself from realizing the state. For the question presupposes a method or system, which there is not, and also that effort can achieve the desired result, which it cannot; and anyway, to desire a result is another disqualifier. So to the age-old question, what must a man do to be saved or to attain perfection, enlightenment, liberation, or to become godlike? Krishnamurti answered that there is nothing he can do. If this seems a melancholy message it must be understood that all doing is an activity of thought, which is bondage, and therefore to be free one must go by the path of not-doing, which is no easy task with the mischievous, chattering mind that man is endowed with. Although he declined to teach any system or method, Krishnamurti had a great deal to say about how, through meditation, the mind may become silent. This is a subject we shall take up in a later chapter, in the context of a discussion of the psychological revolution which Krishnamurti maintained must occur if unregenerate man is not to destroy himself and his world.

11

On Life and Death

LIFE is one thing, and living is quite another, and most of our problems, frustrations and dissatisfactions occur because our living is out of phase with the movement of life. Krishnamurti compared life to a great river, deep and wide, which flows continuously and steadily, in which there is always movement and activity. He compared living, as it is for most people, to a little pool lying beside the river and unconnected with it, in which there is no movement at all and the water is stagnant. What most appear to want, he said, is 'little stagnant pools of existence away from life'.[6] The reason why they want this pool-existence is that they are more concerned with security or permanency than they are with life. In point of fact there is no security or permanency, so what they do in effect is forsake the real for the illusory.

Change, death and rebirth are the essential processes of life, observable in all the phenomena of nature, even in the cells of our own bodies, yet people generally resent and seek to resist change and death. They seek security and permanency in family, property, status, reputation, habit, the observance of tradition and religion. By circumscribing their lives with these ephemera they cut themselves off from the flow of life, with the consequence that they become insensitive, dull, and prone to all kinds of problems. But if we come to terms with the facts of change, death and rebirth, or rather learn to find a joy in the sense of being a part of this immutable process of life; if we get out of our pool-existence and push out into the middle of the river, what happens? Then, said Krishnamurti,

life has an astonishing way of taking care of you, because then there is no taking care on your part. Life carries you where it will because you are part of itself; then there is no problem of security, of what people say or don't say, and that is the beauty of life.[6]

Krishnamurti taught the fundamental Buddhist principle that 'all of life is one', that all living things and processes are bound together in relationship. 'Living means relationship', he wrote, 'relationship means contact; contact means cooperation.'[13] But relationship must be a spontaneous process, a vital thing, which it often is not in human living because spontaneity gets hampered by thought. 'Have concepts any kind of significance in relationship?' he asked, implying that they have not. 'But the only relationship we have is conceptual ... There is an *actual* daily living and a conceptual living.'[13] In other words, our relationships with people and with things are generally based on images. People form images of one another as a result of the experiences they have of each individual over the course of time, and in every encounter they tend to react to the image rather than respond to the person. This is particularly true of marriage relationships, and Krishnamurti suggested a basic reason why many marriages fail or become dull when he asked: 'If I do not die to the *image* of myself and to the *image* of my wife, how can I love?'[12]

So again, the obstacles to authenticity are time and memory. Even a marvellous experience of spontaneous love, when it becomes a memory, can be an image that destroys relationship in the present. Krishnamurti proposed as a definition of the word relationship: 'to respond accurately'. So long as we respond to another person according to the image we have of him or her, we are not responding accurately, which means with care, with understanding and love. When people respond to each other inaccurately, according to an image, on the basis of past experiences of pleasure, hurt, desire, impatience, fear, disappointment, disgust, or whatever, there is really no relationship, there is isolation; and in isolation there is no life.

Another thing which militates against the establishment and maintenance of vital relationships between people is the tendency for them to be based on dependence and mutual gratification, to be a kind of trading of qualities, perhaps based on the idea of complementarity – the partners to the relationship make up for each other's deficiencies so that together they constitute a whole, although individually they are partial, incomplete. The incentive to the formation of such relationships is the need for security, not for experience of the fullness of life, so they lead to lives that are really little pool-existences *a deux*, cut off from the river of life. Such pools can spawn all kinds of anti-life attitudes and behaviour, for instance the man who is ruthless and cruel in business, who tries to compensate by being loving and generous to his children, or the man who avoids the real world, seeking in his home and family a refuge from reality.

The principle that there is relationship between all things leads to the further point that Krishnamurti expressed in the title of one of his books, *You Are the World*. For all its emphasis on states of consciousness, Krishnamurti's is not a solipsistic or socially irrelevant philosophy. 'I think we have to understand', he wrote,

> that we are the world and the world is us. The world is each one of us; to feel that, to be really committed to it and to nothing else, brings about a feeling of great responsibility and an action that must not be fragmentary, but whole.[13]

So to deplore the mess that the world is in is an act of self-criticism, which should awaken self-awareness and lead to transformation, both in the individual and, by extension, in society.

In the world, in relationships and societies, conflict appears to be an inalienable factor of life. We may deplore and dissociate ourselves from conflict in the form of war between nations or ideologies, or when it gets out of hand in relationships and leads to grievous violence, but it is difficult for us to conceive of life without conflict. Probably most people believe that up to a point conflict is a good thing, in that it gives zest to life, fosters growth and creativity, and that without it life would be unconscionably dull. But such assumptions, Krishnamurti argued, are mere ideas, and we too readily accept that conflict is fundamental to life, despite the fact that it brings pain and sorrow to our personal lives and in the world at large produces the appalling horrors of war, threatening ultimately to destroy humanity. 'Conflict', he wrote, 'must be understood, not ennobled or suppressed.'[3] The questions, 'How does it originate?' and 'Can we live without it?' must be examined carefully.

Conflict arises from duality, in particular the duality engendered in the mind of man by the contrast between the fact of what is and the idea of what should be. When an individual aspires to become something or not to be something, when he seeks to fulfil a desire or a project, when in relationship he looks to the other to be, become or do something to conform with his ideal or desire, then conflict arises. Human beings are perpetually riven by states of inward conflict, of which they are often unaware: these inward states manifest outwardly in disruptions of relationships and society. There is the brute conflict arising from coveting what another has, be it territory, wealth or status, and there is the idealist's conflict which comes of aspiring to change something for the better, be it the self, others, or the world. Morally, we may regard the former as evil and the latter as good, but both can give rise to violence. Do we imagine that at least things are achieved through conflict, that without it there would be no progress or creation? Would we argue that in order to be and act in the world we must have purposes and projects, conceive and seek results, and that so to do is not necessarily based on dualistic thinking? Krishnamurti conceded that this is true of practical and material projects, like building a house or a bridge. But action with a plan or purpose in relation to the self, another, others, or society, is a different matter. The conflict that such action engenders is not creative, it can never bring the new into being, because plans and purposes are only conceived in terms of the known, of past experience. So all action and conflict based on such plans is as futile as the activity of a dog chasing its own tail.

Can there, then, be such a thing as action without a purpose? Given that life is inconceivable without action, must that action necessarily involve conflict? Can we live without conflict? Krishnamurti would answer that the only effective action is action without a purpose, free of the directives of the self or an idea, and that to live without conflict, in harmony with 'what is', is not only possible but is the only way we can get out of our stagnant pool-existences and into the flow of life.

The fact is that most of us live in conflict of one kind or another, and accept conflict as a necessary part of the human condition. We may try to end it, by getting ourselves psychoanalysed, or divorced, or entering into contracts or treaties, but these are really only stratagems for avoiding conflict, and they notoriously don't end it. Of course, to seek to end it is to act with a purpose and thus give rise to further conflict. So is man doomed to be in a state of perpetual conflict, and therefore to be cut off from life? If conflict cannot be ended by thought, by analysis, by seeking out its causes and trying to eradicate them, have we no alternative but to acquiesce in it as an inalienable factor of life, to accept as the human lot all the individual and collective suffering that such acquiescence entails? That would be to accept the poverty and littleness of our living as compared with the richness and magnificence of life, to settle for a stultified dualism for ever divorced from the oneness and flow of life. There is an alternative, Krishnamurti said. Conflict cannot be ended, but it can come to an end. If we are intelligently aware of it in all its manifestations, if we observe it whenever it arises, do not try to suppress, judge or analyse it, but just watch it, turn upon it 'the flame of attention', which is awareness uncorrupted by the sense of the self, conflict comes to an end.

That conflict alientates us from life is a proposition more generally and readily assented to than the proposition that pleasure also does. If conflict and pain are the negative side of life, pleasure and enjoyment are surely its positive side; certainly they are what most people live for. In the West we have enough experience, historically, of the self-righteousness, the hypocrisy and tyranny of pleasure-denying puritanism to mistrust anyone who speaks out against pleasure or questions the rights of individuals to enjoy it according to their wish, provided their enjoyment does not infringe the liberties of others. We may concede that excess is reprehensible, that a life dedicated to pleasure is deplorably self-indulgent, but most of us have neither the inclination nor the opportunity for such dedication. We consider that the pleasures we have in life counterbalance its pains and burdens and are ultimately what makes life worthwhile. Krishnamurti would ask us to question this attitude. He was no puritan – often in his writings he deplored the excesses of zealots who sought to suppress their own or others' pleasures. We know from his biography and his *Journal* that his own life was certainly not devoid of enjoyment, that he took pleaure both in common human activities, like driving a superb car, telling jokes, dressing smartly, and in the rarer personal experiences that he had of joy in observing and responding to the natural world. So we know that when he asks us to examine our pleasures, and the satisfactions they give, he is not implying that they are reprehensible or sinful, but rather that they are too limited and limiting, that it is not life without pleasure that he is advocating but rather a joy in life that transcends pleasure.

'Let us observe the whole movement of pleasure,' he wrote:

> There is not only biological, including sexual, pleasure, there is also pleasure in possessions, pleasure in having money, pleasure in achieving something that you have been working towards; there is pleasure in power, political or religious, in power over a person; there is

pleasure in the acquisition of knowledge, and in the expression of that knowledge as a professor, as a writer, as a poet; there is the gratification that comes about through leading a very strict, moral and ascetic life, the pleasure of achieving something inwardly which is not common to ordinary man.[20]

The point about all these pleasures is that they are of the ego, they give the self security, substance, status; and they involve thought and the mind, time and continuity. Pleasure-seeking, like seeking anything, is doomed to disappointment, because thought, governed by experience and expectation, has already formulated the end-result of the quest, so nothing new or surprising is going to materialize. The point is not that pleasure is wrong, but that once one has experienced true joy in life, pleasure seems by comparison a shallow and trivial satisfaction.

If not pleasure, what then endows life with meaning and purpose? We may experience joy, cosmic consciousness and the dissolution of the self in such experiences, and still we may ask this question of ourselves, of philosophers or those we regard as the wise or enlightened. Great literature abounds with accounts of man's existential *Angst*, and some people get distressed, even to the point of suicide, if they find the question of the ultimate significance and purpose of life unanswerable. Krishnamurti's view was that the question *is* unanswerable, that 'constantly to seek the purpose is one of the odd escapes of man'[8] from the insecurity and uncertainties of life, and from the realization, which is hard to accommodate to the conditions of normal living and attitudes to living, that 'all life is in the present, not in the shadow of yesterday or in the brightness of tomorrow's hope'.[8] People actually speak of *giving* life meaning or significance. Amazingly, they say it without any sense of irony, although the very expression is an admission that this significance is a creation of thought:

> When you say, 'I have no significance, there is no significance in life', it is thought that has made you say there is no significance, because you want significance. But when there is no movement of thought, life is full of significance. It has tremendous beauty.[17]

The perception and experience of significance comes of really understanding and feeling that 'you are the world', of having become completely divested of all the superficial trappings of selfhood and free of all the fears and anxieties of self-centredness, that you can commit yourself to the flow of the river of life and go along with it. But this also means going along with and being nonanxious about the fact of death. Living and dying go together, said Krishnamurti, they are not two separate things, and 'so one must enquire what it means to die, because that is part of our living'.[13]

We sometimes think of death as the ultimate obscenity, contemplating with horror the time when we will, as Shakespeare put it, 'lie in cold corruption and rot'. We feel that death negates life, that even in prospect it robs life of meaning and purpose, mocks the futility of all our efforts and the ephemerality of all our joys. We may seek to dignify ourselves in the face of it with ceremonies, monuments or memorials, but death is not in turn mocked by such stratagems, and indeed the grander we make our memorials the more we compromise our dignity in the face of death. Krishnamurti insisted that he wanted 'none of that nonsense' associated with his own death. In the last entry in his last *Journal*, written just two years before he died, he recalled witnessing a cremation on a beach in India. There was some weeping and some chanting, but the ceremony was minimal. Simply:

> They carried the father to the beach where they had already collected a great pile of wood and they laid the body on top of that heap of wood and set it on fire. It was all so natural so extraordinarily simple: there were no flowers, there was no hearse, there were no black carriages with black horses. It was all very quiet and utterly dignified.[24]

That was how it should be, natural, because 'everything on earth, on this beautiful earth, lives, dies, comes into being and withers away',[24] and life is not negated but enriched and affirmed by death. Our living cannot be in phase with the movement of life unless we accept death, not abstractly, as something we concede as natural and therefore reconcile ourselves to, but positively, as 'something to be with day in and day out' rather than something to be postponed or put out of mind.

What can it mean, to live with death day in and day out? Medieval monasteries had charnel houses, where the skulls and bones of erstwhile occupants were indecorously stacked to keep the living mindful of death. But the implication there was that life is short and inconsequential and that what alone matters is the fate of the eternal soul. People of religious persuasion have lived with death, and embraced their own deaths, prompted by beliefs that negated life and the physical, natural world. We rightly regard such conduct as misguided and morbid. Of course, when Krishnamurti spoke of living with death day in and day out he was not advocating a cautionary mindfulness of death, but he could easily be misconstrued.

'How can we learn to die?' was a question he was asked on one occasion in India, and he replied, 'I say first learn how to live.'[15] When a person really learns how to live, he maintained, death ceases to be a problem for him and he does not seek solace in some concept of survival. Nor does he fear death. People may fear what they know, but to fear the unknown is illogical and foolish, and death is, supremely, the unknown. Fear of death, then, is not really fear of the unknown, but of losing the known. We tend to think of death, if we think of it at all, as a monstrous thing waiting to pounce upon us at the end of life's journey. If we bring it closer, if we understand that it is an integral part of life and living and there is nothing permanent except life itself, and if we learn in our living continually to die to the old in order to enable the new to exist, we do not fear death.

Religions generally postulate some kind of continuity as the answer to the question of death, offering believers the prospect of reincarnation, resurrection, or survival in some form which, although non-corporeal, is somehow capable of sensory contact with the physical world. But, Krishnamurti argued, thinking in terms of continuity is thinking in terms of time, and the only kind of immortality we can have is in emancipation from time, which is a creation of thought:

> Thought, memory, is continuous through word and repetition. The ending of thought is the beginning of the new; the death of thought is life eternal. There must be constant ending for the new to be. That which is new is not continuous; the new can never be within the field of time. The new is only in death from moment to moment.[4]

Here we come back to the experience of primary importance in Krishnamurti's life and philosophy: the experience of the death of the self. 'What is it that dies?'[18] he asked. The body dies, of course, but that is such a palpable fact that people generally accept it, although they do not so easily accept the ending of the individual personality, the self. If, however, we are persuaded by Krishnamurti's argument that the self is an inconsequential, rather arbitrary, thing, a creation of environment, time, thought and memory, and if, through that understanding or through some experience, we are able to free ourselves from the concept of the self, then we will understand what death is and will not be afraid of it. We will learn to see it as 'a great act of purgation',[18] as a liberation from the ephemeral pleasures, sorrows and attachments of what we call living. 'Can I live with death all the time?' Krishnamurti asked. He explained how it is possible and the consequences of such a mode of living:

> I am attached to you; end that attachment, which is death – is it not? One is greedy, and when one dies one cannot carry greed with one; so end the greed, not in a week's time or ten days' time – end it now. So one is living a life full of vigour, energy, capacity, observation, seeing the beauty of the earth and also the ending of that instantly, which is death. So to live before death is to live with death; which means that one is living in a timeless world.[18]

12

The Psychological Revolution

KRISHNAMURTI lived through a time and in a world of unprecedented social and political turmoil. He saw wars and revolutions claim millions of human lives, he witnessed social and technological changes bewilder people in the present, making them fear for the future. Also, particularly in his native India, he observed societies in the throes of self-destruction through their rigid adherence to traditional modes of thought and conduct. A lot was written in his lifetime about new societies, brave new worlds, Utopias and total revolutions. In many places in the world ideas as to how these fundamental changes might be achieved were put into practice. Such changes as there have been, however, have been superficial: brave new worlds have all too often turned out to be the flip-side of the bad old worlds and to have a tendency to flip back. For all our efforts and awareness there has been little alleviation of human suffering and misery, little mitigation of human destructiveness, cruelty and stupidity, and today, with the dangers of wars on the one hand and ecological catastrophes on the other, there is as much alarmist talk about the end of the world or of human civilization as there ever has been, and not without reason.

In the early 1950s Krishnamurti was asked why he thought that the crisis in the world at that time was exceptional. He gave three reasons. First, because world conflicts were not over territorial or economic issues, but were over ideas, and ideologues were the most ruthless murderers who would make or demand any sacrifice in the cause of their chimerical ideal. Second, because man and the value of human life had ceased to be important to world political leaders, who could contemplate with equanimity the destruction of millions of people if they could see political advantage in it. Third, because of the exaggerated value and importance that man was giving to material values and particularist loyalties, for such a mental attitude was at the basis of human violence and hatred. These circumstances, Krishnamurti said, constituted an unprecedented crisis which demanded an unprecedented solution: nothing less than a psychological revolution, a fundamental change in the human mind and nature.

Revolution is a key term in Krishnamurti's philosophy. What people generally call revolution, he argued, is merely modified continuity, however much blood is shed and suffering undergone in the cause of it. Revolutions involving changes in political systems inevitably fail, 'because a system cannot transform man; man always transforms the system, which history shows'.[2] Gradual political reform, as distinct from revolution, is also unavailing because reform always needs further reform, and is an endless process 'like trying to clean the water in a tank which is constantly being filled with dirty water'.[2] Revolution based on religious beliefs and dogmas must also fail because it involves the exercise of authority and the denial of freedom, thus engendering conflict, both in the individual and in society, which only makes confusion worse. So is revolution itself a chimera? Is it unrealistic to look for change? Must we not accept man's unregenerate nature and leave the matter to God, meanwhile living as moral and honest a life as we can in the circumstances?

Of course, Krishnamurti never proposed such a resigned and negative attitude. He believed that a revolution is not only essential but also possible. He did not minimize the problem. Indeed, he maintained that 'our problems – social, environmental, political, religious – are so complex that we can only solve them by being simple ... These problems demand a new approach; and they can be so approached only when we are simple, inwardly really simple.' This simplicity is not simple-mindedness or stupidity, but the ridding of the mind of all the ideas and so-called knowledge that block the direct perception and experience of reality. 'Our social structure is very intellectual;' he wrote, 'we are cultivating the intellect at the expense of every other factor of our being and therefore we are suffocating with ideas.'[12]

Problems, though, do not yield to attack by ideas, because ideas prevent us seeing a problem in its entirety and in all its ramifications. It is only when there is such seeing and understanding that change comes about, and this involves being simple in

Krishnamurti's sense of the term. In another context he spoke of poverty rather than simplicity, and said: 'It is important to be poor, not only in the things of the world but also in belief and knowledge. A man with worldly riches or a man rich in knowledge and belief will never know anything but darkness, and will be the centre of all mischief and misery.'[2]

Murder, war, genocide, starvation, child-abuse, torture and violence of all kinds are things that we all know occur in the world. We deplore and abhor them, but most of us do not feel in any way associated with them or responsible for them. We distance them, see them as things that occur 'out there', in a world that is incomprehensible to us in its inhumanity. And of course few of us have ever been directly involved in these things. But Krishnamurti insisted that we are all involved and responsible, that the outside world is as it is because of what we are inwardly. 'If we are petty, jealous, vain, greedy – *that* is what we create about us, *that* is the society in which we live.'[12] The atrocities and stupidities perpetrated by nations and faiths may be writ so large that they seem something different from the little meannessess and follies of the individual. But the difference is of degree not of kind, and it is at the level of the individual life that all the trouble starts; there is no other reality, no malevolent devil urging man to do evil against his better nature.

Human qualities and characteristics become manifest in relationships, and human societies are complexes of relationships, so it is in relationships that we can see how things have gone wrong and possibly seek to make them go right. Krishnamurti wrote:

> If you and I do not understand ourselves, merely transforming the outer, which is a projection of the inner, has no significance whatsoever; that is, there can be no significant alteration or modification in society so long as I do not understand myself in relationship to you. Being confused in my relationship, I create a society which is the replica, the outward expression of what I am.[2]

So the only revolution that could change the world is a revolution in the individual and in his attitudes to, and conduct in, his relationships, not only with other people but also with things, with nature, and with ideas.

Relationships must be vital, which means that they must be sustained by an investment of energy. Mechanical energy is subject to the law of entropy, it runs down, the operations it governs become increasingly random, and ultimately it results in a static state. This is an established fact of physical science which can be applied by analogy to society and the relationships which constitute it. If those relationships are sustained by habit, tradition, pragmatic or politic considerations formulated by thought, then they are mechanical, subject to randomness, and will settle in a static form. But science recognizes another kind of energy than the mechanical, which is 'negentropic', that is to say, it does not run down but goes on indefinitely and supports increasingly complex organic structures. This is the fundamental life energy: when it functions in relationships it makes those relationships vital instead of mechanical, and that vitality invests the social structure which the complex of relationships comprises.

In a key passage, Krishnamurti put it this way:

> To bring about a society that is not repetitive, not static, not disintegrating, a society that is constantly alive, it is imperative that there should be a revolution in the psychological structure of the individual, for without inward, psychological revolution, mere transformation of the outer has little significance ... Outward action, when accomplished, is over, is static; if the relationship between individuals, which is society, is not the outcome of inward revolution, then the social structure, being static, absorbs the individual and therefore makes him equally static, repetitive ... It is a fact that society is always crystallising and absorbing the individual and that constant, creative revolution can only be in the individual, not in the outer. That is, creative revolution can take place only in individual relationship, which is society.[2]

A vital relationship is one in which there is love. Krishnamurti often spoke and wrote about love, and the term is central to his thinking about the psychological revolution, so let us see what he meant by it.

In attempting to define love, he proceeded by way of stating what it is not, because 'as love is the unknown, we must come at it by discarding the known'. He first rejected the love that is possessive, for it gives rise to jealousy, fear and conflict. Then he considered whether to love is to be emotional and sentimental. He rejected the idea because emotion and sentimentality are merely forms of self-expansion: when emotion is frustrated or sentiment is not responded to a person may become cruel and violent, even towards the person he professes to love. The next supposed loving quality to come under scrutiny was forgiveness. Krishnamurti rejected the claim of the forgiving person to be loving on the grounds that to say 'I forgive you' is to give undue importance to the 'I', to make the self the important figure in the situation. Forgiveness, sympathy, sentiment, jealousy, possessiveness, are all of the mind, 'as long as the mind is the arbiter, there is no love'. But 'when these things disappear, when these things don't occupy your mind and when the things of the mind don't fill your heart, then there is love; and love alone can transform the present madness and insanity in the world'.[2]

Love, in other words, only comes into being with the death of the self. It is not a creation or activity of the self, not something we can practise or cultivate, and above all it is not something that seeks results, for such seeking is a function of the mind, of the self, implying time, and love is not of time or of the self. Although it does not seek results, it is the only thing that can vitalize the relationships of which society is built up, and therefore the only thing that can produce the result of transforming society.

Of course, much of this has been said before. The poet W. H. Auden put it even more plainly when he wrote the line: 'We must love one another or die.' Auden was a Christian poet, and of course this is the basic Christian message. But Krishnamurti did not merely prescribe in vague terms the remedy for the world's ills; he went into precise detail as to how the psychological revolution might come about. Here we come to what is most original and most contentious in the teaching: the claim that the change can be virtually instantaneous.

A notable social development in the 1970s was the emergence and consolidation of the 'human potentials movement', which comprised numerous organizations and individuals advocating various means of promoting human spiritual growth and the full use of latent capacities. Although it had its fringe of faddists and fools, it reflected a widespread awareness of the need for radical change both in the individual and society. Undoubtedly many people profited by it, in that they learnt to live what they considered more fulfilling and meaningful lives. Krishnamurti however, looked rather askance at the movement, for he did not believe that radical psychological change is a cumulative process, the outcome of a programme of growth. He was not an evolutionist, but a revolutionist. 'Transformation is not in the future . . . It can only be *now*,' he wrote. 'Regeneration is today, not tomorrow.'[2] All means of seeking and working at change are activities of the self; radical change is not a matter of the self becoming something other, but of the self coming to an end, and that has to happen instantaneously.

How does it happen? Krishnamurti returned to this question many times over the years, and à propos it developed his thoughts on 'the art of seeing'. He asked, 'What do we mean by transformation?' and answered:

> Surely it is very simple: seeing the false as the false and the true as the true. Seeing the truth in the false and seeing the false in that which has been accepted as truth. Seeing the false as the false and the true as the true is transformation, because when you see something very clearly as the truth, that truth liberates. When you see that something is false, that false thing drops away.[5]

In this passage, seeing could be read as synonymous with understanding. But elsewhere Krishnamurti made it quite clear that the seeing that leads to transformation is also seeing in the quite literal sense of the term. To observe, he said, 'is quite an art, to which one must give a good deal of attention'.[2] We only see very partially, we never see anything completely, with the totality of our mind, or with the fullness of our heart. Conditioning, concern with our own problems, our tendency to conceptualize, to form images of people and things, thereafter seeing the image instead of the reality, all prevent our direct perception of 'what is'. Also our training and cultural background have taught us to see fragmentarily, analytically, to see the parts separately rather than the totality which they constitute. This kind of seeing leads to dullness and insensitivity, to the mentality capable of exploiting or hurting the part because it does not see it in relation to the whole.

Total, clear, unimpeded seeing is rare; as rare, indeed, as love. In fact in a sense it is love, for genuine love cannot exist without it. In such seeing there is no barrier between the observer and the observed. People who have taken psychoactive drugs have experienced this breaking down of barriers, or contraction of the space between observer and observed. But, said Krishnamurti, it is not necessary to take drugs:

> There is a much simpler, more direct, more natural way, which is to observe for yourself a tree, a flower, the face of a person; to look at any one of them, and so to look that the space between them and you is non-existent. And you can only look that way when there is love.[13]

As with seeing, so with listening:

> Listen to the birds, listen to your wife's voice, however irritating,

beautiful or ugly, listen to it and listen to your own voice however beautiful, ugly or impatient it may be. Then out of this listening you will find that all separation between the observer and the observed comes to an end.[13]

Listening and seeing are modes of attention. Attention is another word that Krishnamurti used with special significance. We speak of paying attention and, largely as a result of our schooling, we think of attention as a disciplining of the mind, forcing it to concentrate on a particular thing to the exclusion of other things, resisting distraction. We tend to think that the mind can only be in one of two states, either wandering, open to all kinds of vagrant thoughts and impressions, or concentrated, absorbed by one thing.

Krishnamurti maintained that these are not the only possible mental states, that there is another mode of attention which is not absorbed and exclusive. Being absorbed, forcing attention and resisting distraction, are things that misuse energy which would be better applied to unforced and non-exclusive attention. Such attention *is* discipline. The Latin root of the word discipline, Krishnamurti pointed out, means to learn, and learning is not something forced but something accomplished through observation. For the mind which is choicelessly constantly aware, which is attentive and responsive to impressions from the totality of its environment from moment to moment, learning is a natural and continuous process. Truth is accessible to such a mind, but it is not accessible to the mind that is concentrated on one thing, even if that thing is the pursuit of truth, or to the mind that is crammed with knowledge, belief and experience.

In the 'human potentials movement' there are many purveyors of techniques of meditation and mind control, and Krishnamurti observed with a kind of amusement the success and popularity they enjoyed in the 1970s. 'Unfortunately', he told one of his audiences:

> people come from the East with their systems, methods and so on; they say 'Do this' and 'Don't do that', 'Practise Zen and you will find enlightenment'. Some of you may have gone to India or Japan and spent years studying, disciplining yourself, trying to become aware of your toe or your nose, practising endlessly. Or you may have repeated certain words in order to calm the mind, so that in that calmness there will be the perception of something beyond thought. These tricks can be practised by a very stupid, dull mind. I am using the word stupid in the sense of a mind that is stupefied. A stupefied mind can practise any of those tricks.[11]

These 'tricks' are supposed to be systems of meditation, but, said Krishnamurti,

> a system implies practice, following, repetition, changing 'what actually is' and therefore increasing your conflict. Systems make the mind mechanical, they don't give you freedom, they may promise freedom at the end, but freedom is at the beginning not at the end.[13]

To practise meditation for the purpose of self-improvement, in the hope of advancing spiritually, or of becoming a more relaxed person, and therefore happier and more efficient, involves pursuing aims in time. But real meditation is a way of being, not of becoming, and it is impossible for a mind that is seeking results. 'Freedom is at the beginning,' said Krishnamurti, and elsewhere he stated that 'the first step is the last step'. He did not offer a technique for bringing about the instantaneous psychological transformation in the individual, which he maintained was the only revolution that would guarantee humanity a future in the world, but what he had to say about meditation gave clear guidance on the subject, and is really the very essence of his teaching. 'A psychological revolution', he wrote,

> is absolutely necessary for a different kind of world, a different kind of society to come into being; and that revolution can only take place at the very centre of our being and requires a great abundance of energy; meditation is the release of that total energy.[2]

People who meditate according to a prescribed system or method usually set apart certain times of day for the practice and do it under special conditions. But, said Krishnamurti, meditation has no beginning and no end, it is not something you can do deliberately. 'Don't look out of the window hoping to catch it unawares, or sit in a darkened room waiting for it; it comes only when you are not there at all, and its bliss has no continuity.[8]

Krishnamurti was emphatic about what meditation is not. It is not an escape from the world, it is not 'the repetition of a word, nor the experience of a vision, nor the cultivation of silence . . . not wrapping yourself in a pattern of thought, in the enchantment of pleasures'.[8] It is not prayer, for the prayer that is supplication is born of self-pity, which is rooted in the sense of separateness. In the meditative experience there is no separateness, there is wholeness and union with the whole movement of life. And it is not a way or a path to anything, certainly not to freedom, for freedom is the precondition of true meditation.

Krishnamurti certainly did not make it easy for anyone who wished to embark on the work which he stressed is essential to the world's survival. But while he insisted that there is no 'how' of meditation, his talks and writings are full of indications as to the conditions and attitudes conducive to meditation in his sense of the term. Perhaps he was least ambiguous about it when he was talking to children. In one such talk he told his audience:

> You have to watch, as you watch a lizard going by, walking across the wall, seeing all its four feet, how it sticks to the wall, you have to watch it, and as you watch you see all the movement, the delicacy of its movements. So in the same way, watch your thinking, do not correct, do not suppress it – do not say it is too hard – just watch it, now, this morning.[30]

The basis of meditation, then, is watchfulness, both of the objective and the subjective worlds. It is 'seeing, watching, listening, without word, without comment, without opinion – attentive to the movement of life in all its relationships throughout the day'. It is the continual emptying of the mind of thought and experience, allowing the stream of consciousness to flow freely without thought seizing on any of its elements; it is living and dying from moment to moment.

Another paradox about it is that although it is not a thing you can deliberately set out to do, it nevertheless demands hard work and 'the highest form of discipline – not conformity, not obedience, but a discipline which comes through constant awareness, not only of the things about you outwardly, but also inwardly'.[8] Just watch and be aware of all your thoughts, feelings and reactions, without judging, comparing, approving, condemning or evaluating them in any way, Krishnamurti said. Try it, do it, he urged, and you will find that there is a tremendous release of energy, there is the opening of the door into spaciousness, there is the awakening of bliss.

In a telling image, he likened the bliss of meditation to a pure flame, and thought to the smoke from a fire which brings tears to the eyes and blurs perception. In meditation the mind penetrates and understands the entire structure of the self and the world that thought has put together; and the very act of seeing and understanding confers freedom from it, for meditation 'destroys everything, nothing whatsoever is left, and in this vast, unfathomable emptiness there is creation and love'.[6]

PART THREE

•

Developments and Applications

13

Living and Learning

WHETHER or not Krishnamurti was the World Teacher, he was certainly a great educationist and an exemplary school teacher, and he set more value by the latter role than the former. During his sojourns at the schools in India, England and California he had frequent long discussions with the students and teachers about education and its significance in life. The schools – or as he preferred to call them, 'educational centres' – were where the philosophy was brought down to earth and put into practice. Adults might protest the difficulty of applying its principles in their own lives, but the schools were where its relevance and applicability were demonstrable. The world has been brought to a parlous state by the prevailing systems of education, which fostered careerism, competition, authoritarianism, conformism and specialization. Krishnamurti believed that if a saner and safer world were to come about these biases would have to be expunged from its educational systems. The schools associated with his name were to show that this could be done. 'It is our responsibility as educators', he wrote in one of his open *Letters to the Schools*, 'to bring about a mind that has no conflict within itself and so end the struggle and conflict in the world about us.' This may sound optimistic, but we have to remember that whatever Krishnamurti did he did because he saw clearly that it was the right thing to do, and not with any expectation of results. He certainly did not expect the alumni of the Krishnamurti schools to go out and change the world, but he saw clearly that the world needed a revolution in the principles and practice of schooling, and that revolution had to begin somewhere.

In most people's experience, school is a place of conflict. There are disciplines imposed, rules are laid down and their infringements punished, rewards and penalties are meted out for achievements or failures in academic or sports performances, students vie with each other, form themselves into aggressively competing gangs or coteries, teachers impose work-loads and parents pressurize. All this goes on at a time when a young person is coping with the common adolescent conflicts involving sexuality, self-confidence and relating to others and the world. School is where the behavioural patterns are established both for those who go under and those who scramble to the top of the heap. Schools are noisy, competitive, tough, restless, demanding, crowded places – just like the world at large. However competent they may be at educating, they are certainly places of learning: where we learn our competencies and inadequacies, how to adapt to or fit into the world, to be leader or led, winner or loser in the struggle of life.

The Krishnamurti schools are totally different. For a start, they are all set in beautiful environments. The English one at Brockwood in Hampshire is in a large Georgian mansion, surrounded by its own gardens and parkland. The school generally has its full complement of sixty students, aged from fourteen to the mid-twenties, and there are about thirty staff members. Except when they all congregate for meals the visitor to Brockwood would not know there were so many people there. The first impression one has is of quietness, of students and staff unhurriedly and quietly going about their business. The tasks of tidying, cleaning, gardening, washing dishes and so on, are shared by students and staff alike. There is a principal, but his task is conceived as coordinator rather than 'head', and he receives the same salary as other staff members. All decisions are taken after consultation with the staff or the entire school, as appropriate.

There is a daily routine which has been established by agreement on the principle that the school is a community and its efficient running requires it. The day begins at 7.30 with a short morning meeting when the school assembles to sit in silence or listen to a poem or a piece of music that someone has brought. Breakfast and household tasks precede classes, which run from 9 am until 1 pm. Lunch is followed by a rest period, then there are more classes, sports or other activities from 3 pm to 7 pm. After supper students do homework or socialize, and by 10 pm they are in their rooms preparing for bed. The students are of both sexes, and come from all over the world. Classes cater to their varying interests and needs, and the curriculum includes preparation for university entrance and other examinations.

Academic achievement in a subject is not pursued for its own sake but rather is expected to be incidental to the student's engaged exploration of the subject, which includes exploration of how it relates to other subject areas and, more generally, to life and the world at large. There is no direct teaching of Krishnamurti's philosophy, although there are occasional extra-curricular discussions of aspects of it, in which guests often participate and which students may choose to attend or not. The Krishnamurti schools are not dedicated to promulgating their founder's teachings, but rather to incorporating them into their community life and their educational work. The quiet, the orderliness, the shared activities, the friendliness of everyone, and the general atmosphere of a happy community which the visitor observes, suggest that they largely succeed in doing so.

Although Krishnamurti did not lay down a code of conduct for the students at the schools or specific procedures for the teachers, he did, in his many discussions with them, clearly establish general principles and thoroughly explore their implications. These discussions are in themselves examples of educational method, in that Krishnamurti, through patient reasoning and without assuming authority, establishes a comprehensive view of a question and generally elicits consent to his principle.

Adolescents coming from the outside world into a non-authoritarian environment dedicated to fostering their freedom might well have problems, particularly when they are 'expected' to be at a morning meeting by 7.30, to help wash the dishes and do the gardening, and to be in bed by 10 pm. Although students enter the environment of their own free will (none are enrolled on parental decision alone), they are sometimes understandably confused as to where their freedom lies and how the 'expected' differs from the ordained. Krishnamurti always stressed, in his discussions with them, that freedom is not the liberty to do as one likes irrespective of how others are affected, and that in community life it must be modified by consideration, affection, intelligence, and respect for the consensus as to the principles of conduct which made the community work, without energy being dissipated by conflicts over basically trivial matters. 'We are human beings in relationship with each other,' he said, 'therefore we must understand what it means to live together in freedom. And that demands intelligence.'[14] Intelligence implied total awareness of a situation. If, for example, a student was planning to go out for a walk and someone said he was needed in the kitchen, there should not be a conflict between his wish and the other's demand, because the facts of the situation, intelligently assessed, would dictate the right action. Such situations, he told students, would arise every day of their lives, and

> What you will do depends on how you have listened. If you have really listened you will from now on just act on facts only – that's a marvellous thing, you don't know the beauty of it – just on facts. Instead of bringing all your emotional circus into it.[14]

The fact that he urged students to consider above all was that for most of the year school was their home, and a home was a place that had to be cared for by all who lived in it. At one school meeting a student asked why they shouldn't be at liberty to have sexual relationships, and part of Krishnamurti's reply was:

> This place is your home and you are responsible for it, for the house and the garden and for keeping it orderly. And you are responsible to your parents, to the people here, to the neighbours – the whole of it. And naturally people are watching what is going on here . . . So if you want to have a sexual affair with someone here, you have to be fully awake to all the dangers of it, and also to all the possible consequences . . . Here you are told to enquire into conformity, to understand it, to use your minds, your intelligence. Then this sexual problem arises, the sex instinct is aroused in a place where lots of boys and girls are together. What are you going to do? Pursue your biological urge, secretly or openly? Come on, do discuss this.[14]

He urged on the discussion, making the students examine not only the question of responsibility but also their understanding of the nature of sexuality and why for human beings it was so important and such a problem. When one student protested that suppressing it created conflict, Krishnamurti said, 'So you do it, and then what?' There was still conflict. 'This is one of the problems of life and you don't want to face it,' he went on. 'How is your mind going to be intelligent enough to deal with it? How can one bring about a mind that is capable of neither resisting, suppressing or yielding? This is a real problem. This issue will exist right through life.' Only intelligence, he said, could deal with it, so:

> Have an intelligent mind, not a distorted mind. A distorted mind says, 'This is what I want and I'm going after it.' Which means that it has no concern for the whole, but only for its own little demands – it has not been watching the whole process. So here it is your responsibility to

have this intelligence, and if you don't have it, then don't blame anyone else.[14]

Never censorious, but always reasonable and appealing to reason, Krishnamurti managed to convey to students, while discussing specific and often trivial subjects, fundamental principles of his philosophy of life, and to demonstrate that clarity and totality of awareness that it was the schools' purpose to foster. To accomplish the educational work of bringing about minds without conflict required a sustained interrogation of the springs of conflict in particular situations. For most people, adults as well as children, that is such an unfamiliar kind of enquiry that it has to be taught patiently and persistently. The ramifications of the springs of conflict are vast, extending not only throughout interpersonal and community relationships, but also into the fundamentals of conventional educational thinking and practice. To have a motive for learning, to be ambitious, to proceed by way of comparison and competition, are all things that give rise to conflict.

Learning, Krishnamurti insisted, is discovery. The statement is a simple one, but its implications are enormous. If we have a motive for learning, we will very probably accomplish what we seek, but we won't make any discoveries, because the objective of the learning process has already been defined before the process starts. To study in order to acquire a qualification, a degree or competence for a job is not learning, it is processing knowledge, which is a function that in the modern world machines are becoming more efficient at than human beings. Krishnamurti was not against vocational training as an aspect of education; he only insisted that it was not the whole, or even the most important part of it. 'A student,' he told teachers, 'must have an abundance of the known – mathematics, geography, history – and yet be abundantly free of the known, remorselessly free of it.'[26] In schools, authority was not only vested in the relational hierarchy of teachers and students, but also in the corpuses of knowledge being transmitted from the one to the other and enshrined in textbooks. Education, Krishnamurti told students, 'is not only learning from books, memorising some facts, but also learning how to look, how to listen to what books are saying, whether they are saying something true or false'.[26] Learning as it is generally conceived of is a passive thing: the mind, sponge-like, soaks up knowledge, and when it has soaked up enough of it begins to apply it, to act, to exercise the acquired competence. Such learning is mechanical, and never leads to discovery. But real learning is active, it comes through doing, and the mind engaged in it never says 'I know' but rather 'Let's find out', and the process of finding out is never boring or tiring because it is non-mechanical and keeps the mind always alert and fresh. To want to find out is not a motive, it is a passion, a need for and love of truth, and it requires the exercise of intelligence rather than the deployment of knowledge. There is no conflict, no personal ambition, no spirit of competition involved in finding out. Where there is passion these things appear utterly trivial and irrelevant.

'Right education is to help you find out for yourself what you really, with all your heart, love to do,'[25] Krishnamurti said in one of his talks to students. That was the fundamental and most important discovery that educators should be concerned with, for that was the key to fostering minds without conflict. Conflict and discontent are inevitable in life if we don't love what we do. Finding out what you love to do is not the same as finding out what you are good at doing. Conventional education proceeds the latter way, isolating a specific talent, skill or competence and developing it so that it furnishes the foundations for a career or profession. Doing what you are good at may yield satisfaction, but that satisfaction invariably wanes as the doing becomes more mechanical, and there is no freedom from conflict because there is always comparison and competition with someone else who can do it better, or more profitably or successfully. Krishnamurti was not advocating specialization or the cultivation of individual talent, he was saying that if there isn't love and enthusiasm in whatever one does, then the activity is pointless, and right education should emphasize this. 'If you do not help the student to love what he is doing,' he told teachers, 'then he will drift into self-contradiction and despair.'[26] And that love should extend to everything one does, and not be confined to a particular activity or subject. As he said to students at Brockwood:

> To live intelligently implies playing games, looking after the garden, doing things with one's hands, not just with one's brain. Personally, I like to do everything, gardening, milking cows, looking after children, looking after babies, changing diapers – I have done all kinds of things. I like it, nobody imposes it on me, and that's the way to live, that's the most intelligent way.[15]

The emphasis always comes back to the cultivation and use of intelligence as distinct from knowledge. That was Krishnamurti's idea of what the schools were for: to develop the alertness, sensitivity and pliability of mind that constitute intelligence. Intelligence involves critical awareness in relation to everything: the self, the community, the world at large, whatever one is doing or studying. 'Learn never to accept anything which you yourself do not see clearly,'[26] he said, stressing that the seeing must be objective, because 'intelligence has no involvement . . . does not hold on to any particular judgement or evaluation'.[26] To enable students to go into the world equipped with such intelligence was far more important than to send them out crammed with knowledge. But intelligence is not a specific thing that can be taught or learnt, it is not a subject like mathematics. When a student asked, 'How is one to become intelligent?' Krishnamurti replied that the very question implied a concept of what intelligence is, a model which you tried to mould yourself to. 'The moment you try to become intelligent, you cease to be intelligent,' he said,

> whereas, if one is dull and begins to find out what dullness is without any desire to change it into something else, without saying, 'I am dull, stupid, how terrible!' then one will find that in unravelling the problem there comes an intelligence freed of stupidity, and without effort.[6]

Intelligence is not a special faculty or gift, it is a thing that everyone has, only in most people it is smothered: by opinions, beliefs, ambitions, fears, purposes, religious and cultural values, prohibitions and imperatives. For it to appear and operate, all this conditioning has to be stripped away, the mind has to look at it all, clearly and objectively, and negate it. The world being what it is, intelligence begins with and is sustained by denial. Krishnamurti told Brockwood students:

> To live in this insane world sanely, I must reject that world, and a revolution in me must come about so that I become sane and operate sanely . . . That's what education is. You have been sent here, or you have come here, contaminated by an insane world. Don't fool yourselves, you have been conditioned by that insane world, shaped by past generations – including your parents – and you come here and you have to uncondition yourselves, you have to undergo a tremendous change.[14]

The first thing that has to be eliminated before the mind can begin to be free of conditioning is fear. This is one of Krishnamurti's recurrent themes in his talks with students and teachers. Fear is the root both of conflict and of conformity. Most people, as they get older, amass a burden of fears, become 'afraid of living, afraid of losing a job, afraid of tradition, afraid of what the neighbours, or what the wife or husband would say, afraid of death'.[6] In most institutions, the family, the school, the workplace, communities, churches and nations, conformity is enforced by fear. It is fear that makes the world go on in the same appalling way from generation to generation, and if there is to be a significant change in the world it will come about through the activities of a generation liberated from fear. That liberation can begin in the school, if it is a community ordered by the intelligent cooperation of all its members and therefore without authority. In such an environment an individual can examine any fears he or she may have acquired through earlier experience or conditioning; one of the functions of the teacher is to guide and facilitate such an examination. The basic strategy, again, is that of 'finding out why', not overcoming or suppressing fear, but understanding it, and in particular understanding that it is a creation of thought, of the mind grooved in time, distracted from 'what is' by apprehensions about what will or might be. Fear makes people half alive, dissipates mental energy and eventually makes the mind deteriorate. So it is essential that it should be understood and dissolved. As Krishnamurti said in one of his talks to students:

> Fear is what prevents the flowering of the mind, the flowering of goodness ... To be afraid of being nobody, of not arriving, of not succeeding, is at the root of competition. But when there is fear, you cease to learn. And so it seems to me that the function of education is to eliminate fear.[26]

With the elimination of fear, the negation of all other factors of conditioning becomes a relatively easy matter.

Krishnamurti often used the 'flowering of the mind' metaphor when speaking about the aims of education. Conventional education is partial, both in the sense of being biased towards academic or career achievement, and in the sense that it develops only a limited part of the potentials of the mind. If human beings are on the whole violent, selfish, insensitive, callous, dissembling, acquisitive, and if the problems manifested in the world at large are directly attributable to these characteristics, it is the education of the partial mind that is responsible. The partial mind may be stuffed with knowledge and highly capable, but its capacities for seeing, listening and caring are undeveloped, consequently it is a stunted and potentially dangerous mind. It is never quiet, never really aware, never creative, except in spurious clever ways, always preoccupied with its own activities and their relevance. Krishnamurti told students:

> The function of your teachers is to educate not only the partial mind but the totality of the mind; to educate you so that you do not get caught in the little whirlpool of existence but live in the whole river of life. This is the whole function of education. The right kind of education cultivates your whole being, the totality of your mind. It gives your mind and heart a depth, an understanding of beauty.[26]

This idea of the principal function of education demands an unusual kind of teacher, one who himself is a sensitive, aware and whole human being. In his many discussions with teachers at the schools, Krishnamurti often put to them questions like:

> How would you awaken the mind as a whole? It is your problem. How would you see that you are completely alive, inside and outside; in your feelings, in your taste, in everything? And how would you awaken in the student this feeling of non-fragmented living?[26]

The teacher's function was at the same time 'to help the student to see the flowers and also to be very good at mathematics',[26] because one capacity developed to the exclusion of the other produced a partial human being. Teaching and learning, Krishnamurti stressed, are not separate things, and the teacher-student relationship should not be a one-way trafficking of information, but a shared process of exploration and discovery, not only in the classroom and in respect of specific subjects but also out of it and in relation to life as a whole. There is no end to learning, it is a process that goes on throughout life. An important part of human life and communication consists in sharing it, and whether that sharing occurs in school in a designated 'educational' context or in a quite informal life situation is irrelevant. An essential quality in a teacher is to be able to convey his own joy in learning. Krishnamurti asked:

> Is it possible to educate both ourselves and students to live? I do not mean to live merely as an intellectual being but as a complete human being, having a good body and a good mind, enjoying nature, seeing the totality, the misery, the love, the sorrow, the beauty of the world.[26]

Whenever he asked, 'Is it possible...?' the implication was that that was what the schools were about, and if it were not possible they would turn out little different from conventional schools. Perhaps he preferred the term 'educational centres' because it stressed the fact that they were places where everyone was in a learning situation, students and staff alike.

If that were not the case, the schools could not operate in a manner consistent with Krishnamurti's philosophy. Not only is the conventional student-teacher relationship incompatible with that philosophy, but the very idea of education as preparation for something is irreconcilable to it, for it implies a future-orientation, a concern with results and the incentive of a motive. What is really revolutionary in Krishnamurti's educational philosophy is the rejection of the principle of preparation. Students at the schools may take examinations and get qualifications, but these things are incidental, consequences of learning rather than its purpose. Equally revolutionary is the principle that the schools are places of unlearning as well as of learning, that in fact true learning cannot occur until the mind has intelligently unravelled and thereby unlearnt the extent of its conditioning. One could perhaps say that Krishnamurti conceived the deconditioning and consequential 'flowering' of the mind as preparing the student for life; but there was no concept of life as a future state that determined the nature of the flowering. Indeed the term 'flowering' suggests a natural process, not one influenced by external factors, so it would be more apt to speak of the schools' equipping rather than preparing the student for life. Furthermore, Krishnamurti always emphasized that life is the here and now; and for both students and teachers the here and now is the life they live together in the school community. What they learn through confronting and dealing with the problems and situations that arise in the daily life of the community is as essential a part of education as what they learn in the classroom. Equally important is what they learn through playing games, or gardening, or doing the daily chores. 'Everything teaches you,' Krishnamurti said. 'Life itself is your teacher, and you are in a constant state of learning.'[6]

There are at present eight Krishnamurti schools in the world and, although they miss his presence and guidance, they have continued to flourish since his death. Each is independent, but all seek to embody the principles and spirit of Krishnamurti's teaching in their daily lives and learning. Sometimes they cooperate in developing courses, and whenever possible one school will play host to another or others. Many ex-students keep in touch with their former schools, by correspondence or through visits. Many say that the time they spent there brought about a major change in their lives. Some other educational establishments, and many individual teachers throughout the world, have been influenced by their work, and by Krishnamurti's writings and discussions on the subject of education. Whether that influence could extend more broadly into general education, at least to modify, if not entirely to expunge, its biases, remains a moot question. But at a time when the faults and failings of conventional education are becoming more and more manifest and publicized, it would only require a few appropriately placed people to say, 'Let's find out.'

14

Life's Problems

HUMAN life is beset with problems. We have personal problems, interpersonal problems, existential problems, circumstantial problems, social problems, and numerous other kinds. Problems may distress us and get us down, but also, surely, they humanize us, educate us, mature us, enlarge our sympathies and sense of human community. They are the stuff of literature and of much of human discourse, from the book of philosophy to the dinner party conversation. Life puts us to the test with problems: how we tackle, overcome, resolve or cope with them determines our character. We suffer, we agonize, we go under or we pull through – that's life, that's the human condition. If somebody, through privilege or circumspection, avoids it, we consider they must be complacent or insensitive. We admire the achiever, the survivor, the stoic, and our hearts go out to those who are broken, in mind, body or spirit, by life's problems. We can identify with he who overcomes and he who is overcome, but someone who professed not to have problems, or to refuse to have them, would seem to be declaring a dissociation from the human condition and to be either an idiot or a saint.

Krishnamurti said, 'I refuse to have problems' in one of his dialogues with David Bohm.[22] He certainly wasn't an idiot, and we know that he didn't regard himself or wish to be regarded as any kind of saint, so how are we to regard his statement? He would have argued against every sentence in the first paragraph of this chapter, except the first two. His attitude to problems, as to so many things, turned received wisdom and conventional thinking on its head. When people came to him with problems they didn't get any priestly consolations or admonitions, nor did they get the wise man's advice, direction or solution. Some went away disappointed that these expected responses were not forthcoming, but many went away with a changed attitude to and understanding of their problems which was more helpful than any bestowed advice or consolation.

When Krishnamurti said that he personally refused to have problems he meant that he refused to dwell upon, worry or cogitate about life situations. Certainly he conceded that there are situations in life that demand decision and action, but he denied that a decision is something arrived at by thought and then acted upon. Rather, he said, 'the decision acts', giving as an example his dissolving of the Order of the Star in 1929: 'He had an insight; dissolved it. Finished! Why do we need thought?'[22] Thought, worry, solution-seeking, are processes of the mind, and 'the mind is the maker of problems, and so cannot resolve them'.[3] On this principle, of course, Krishnamurti could not give people advice or some verbal formulation for them to take away and think about. He could only seek to foster in them the insight that would enable them to resolve, or dissolve, the problem themselves.

Krishnamurti was well aware of the ambivalance of human beings towards their problems. 'Struggling with a problem,' he wrote, 'is for the majority of us an indication of existence. We cannot imagine life without a problem; and the more we are occupied with a problem, the more alert we think we are.'[3] We are familiar with problems, our minds feed on them and, although we may be distressed by worrying over them, perhaps deep down we fear that we would be even more distressed and lost if we were without them. We revel in analysis, seeking out causes, dredging up subconscious psychic material and submitting it to the scrutiny of our rational consciousness, thereby expecting to find solutions to the problems we have with ourselves or our relationships. We may engage professionals, psychiatrists or counsellors, to do the analysis for us, for we acknowledge that we are complex creatures and that the proper understanding of our complexities requires a particular kind of competence. Other kinds of professional, priests or gurus, minister to our spiritual problems or those that arise from common situations, such as bereavement or confronting our own death. Certainly we want to solve our problems, or to be helped to solve them, but they are so many and varied that we don't expect ever to be free of problems, and probably we are not sure that we would want to be.

Of course not, Krishnamurti would say, because all problems

relate to the self, the unique human being that we each think we are and that, whether we are rather proud of or rather dissatisfied with it, we value for its uniqueness. 'Problems will always exist where the activities of the self are dominant,'[3] he wrote. And one of the activities of the self is to seek solutions to problems. We set up a situation in which the problem and the solution are two separate things, imagining that the one can cancel out the other. We focus on finding a solution, and on arriving at one then apply it or carry it out; and often we generate other problems through our efforts. It is not difficult to find solutions, the human mind is adept at the game, but all this attention directed to the solution really leaves the problem itself unattended to.

> To look for an answer is to avoid the problem – which is just what most of us want to do . . . But to understand a problem is arduous, it demands quite a different approach, an approach in which there is no lurking desire for an answer . . . One must establish right relationship with the problem, which is the beginning of understanding; but how can there be right relationship with a problem when you are only concerned with getting rid of it? . . . Choiceless awareness of the manner of your approach will bring right relationship with the problem. The problem is self-created, so there must be self-knowledge. You and the problem are one, not two separate processes. You are the problem.[3]

To be told, 'You are the problem', that no answer, whether arrived at by yourself or given you by another, is going to solve your problem, and indeed that to seek to solve it at all is futile, is not the kind of helpful wisdom that you look for when, in your distress, you beat a path to the wise or holy man's door. We feel that we are vulnerable in our distress, and when we confide it in someone we consider that there is an unspoken contract entered into whereby the confidant respects that vulnerability, deals gently with it and extends to us his compassion. Whether he be psychiatrist or priest, we expect him to be on our side in our efforts to deal or cope with our problems, and to respond to our confidence with sympathy and, if possible, helpful advice. The refusal of that sympathy and advice would seem a flagrant breach of contract, a betrayal of confidence, a heartless and negative response to an appeal. Krishnamurti was sometimes charged with such derelictions. His answer was in effect that sympathy only served to pander to a problem, and advice to provide a means of circumventing it, so that neither response helped to get at the truth of it. If the truth was unpalatable or brutal, if it came down to a frank, 'You are the problem', he did not consider it was negative or cruel to point it out. He was not in the business of dispensing comfort or answers; his function was to catalyze understanding, to help bring the truth to light.

He was not in fact unsympathetic – unless we understand the term as synonymous with indulgent. A man who was unsympathetic would not be open, as he always was, to discuss people's problems. There is more sympathy and more commitment bestowed by listening than by furnishing answers, and Krishnamurti was an attentive listener. He often told people: listen to your problem, don't try to do anything about it, but just listen and let it tell you its story. By example he showed how listening with total attention throws more light on a problem than any process of analysis. Listening to it means remaining in and with it, letting it reveal itself in its totality, not reduced to a pattern of causes and effects, and without the mind intervening with its busybody tendencies to judge, condemn, win over or transcend. The truths that manifest themselves to attentive listening may not be palatable or comfortable to live with, but to reject them is to opt for living in falsehood and self-deception. For a confidant to assist such an accommodation is not an extension of sympathy but an engagement in complicity with the rejection and falsehood. Krishnamurti would never enter into such a pact, which was why some people found him negative and even cruel.

In his listening he was alert to the earnestness masquerading as seriousness which is not really a serious commitment to truth but a form of preoccupation with the self. An intellectual, a school teacher, told him that he was distressed, as he imagined millions were, by finding that he no longer had any feeling for anything, any delight in the world, or any genuine pity or concern. 'Why is there this gap between the intellect and the heart?' he asked. 'Why have I lost love?' A plaintive question, and indeed, as the man said, a common one, but did it come from the heart, was it serious or just earnest? Part of Krishnamurti's reply was:

> Do you really care that the mind and heart should come together? Aren't you really satisfied with your intellectual capacities? ... You have divided life into the intellect and the heart and you intellectually observe the heart withering away and you are verbally concerned about it. Let it wither away! Live only in the intellect.

The teacher protested, 'But I do have feelings', but Krishnamurti was relentless:

> Aren't those feelings really sentimentality, emotional self-indulgence? . . . *Be* dead to love; it doesn't matter. Live entirely in your intellect . . . And when you live there, what takes place? . . . You say, 'I must have love, and to have it I must cultivate the heart.' But this cultivation is of the mind and so you keep the two always separate. . .

And to the man's question, 'What am I to do?' he answered: 'You can't do anything. Keep out of it! And listen; and see the beauty of that flower.'[8]

Earnest self-accusers by the score came to Krishnamurti over the years asking, 'What am I to do?' and his reply was always, in effect, that the question was evasive, there was nothing to be done. If change were to come about it would be through self-awareness and not self-criticism. 'Be what you are', was his invariable injunction, 'and listen'. To a woman who accused herself of being insensitive and dull, he said: 'The insensitive cannot become the sensitive; all it can do is be aware of what it is, to let the story of what it is unfold.'[3] To a businessman who confessed a nagging discontent with life, he said, 'Stay with the discontent without desiring to pacify it. It is the desire to be undisturbed that must be understood.'[3] To a man who confessed to being consumed with envy he said: 'Having bred envy, desire seeks a state in which there is no envy; both states are the product of desire. Desire cannot bring about fundamental change.'[4] To a rich man, nearing the end of his life, tormented by guilt for having been unloving and ruthless, and who asked whether he should make amends by giving away his wealth, he said:

> What you are to do is not important, but it is essential to be aware of what you *are* doing . . . You do not want to act, and so you keep on asking what to do. You are again being cunning, deceiving yourself, and so your heart is empty . . . Let your heart be empty. Do not fill it with words, with the actions of the mind. Let your heart be wholly empty; then only will it be filled.[3]

The answer always is that self-accusation is not self-knowledge, it can in fact sometimes be a mode of self-congratulation and a way of avoiding the total truth of 'what is' with a kind of specious awareness.

Although Krishnamurti set little store by psychiatry, regarding the patient-doctor relationship as covertly authoritarian and mere adjustment therapy as inadequate and insidious, he did sometimes interrogate people, in the manner of a psychiatrist, to uncover the latent springs of their distress. A school teacher, appalled by the discovery that, although superficially she was affectionate and kindly, there had always been in all her relationships an undercurrent of hate and antagonism, was asked, 'What are you interested in, not professionally, but deep down?'. She said she had always wanted to paint. When asked why she hadn't done so, she spoke about her father, a mercenary and aggressive man, who had insisted that she should take a remunerative job. Krishnamurti probed further, asking if she had been married and had children. She spoke about an affair with a married man, her furious jealousy of his wife and children, which extended, when the affair broke up, to envy of anyone who seemed happily married or successful. By way of compensation, she had tried to become the ideal teacher. Krishnamurti pointed out, that very effort, that pursuit of an ideal, had more deeply suppressed her hate, antagonism and inner conflict. The discussion, up to this point, had more or less followed the psychiatric model, but when the woman said that now she saw it all, recognized and accepted what she actually was, Krishnamurti chided her:

> This very recognition brings a certain pleasure; it gives vitality, a sense of confidence in knowing yourself, the power of knowledge. As jealousy, though painful, gave a pleasurable sensation, so now the knowledge of your past gives you a sense of mastery which is also pleasurable . . . There is pride in knowing, which is another form of antagonism. You are caught in the net of your own thought. How cunning and deceptive it is! It promises release, but only produces another crisis, another antagonism. Just be passively watchful of this and let the truth of it be.[4]

Would she then, the woman asked, be free from jealousy and hate? Krishnamurti answered:

> This desire to gain or to avoid is still within the field of opposition, is it not? See the false as the false, then the truth is . . . Just be passively aware of this total thought-process, and also of the desire to be free of it.[4]

If some people took Krishnamurti's, 'Be what you are' as licence for complacency, they were not allowed to languish in their error for long. Watchfulness is hard work, and the mind is infinitely resourceful in circumventing it by settling for knowledge. Knowledge flatters the self, it permits the illusion of growth and change. Knowledge does not produce action but inertia. A man who protested to Krishnamurti that 'without knowledge we are nothing', was told: 'You are nothing . . . And why not be that? . . . The experiencing of that nothingness is the beginning of wisdom.'[3] He had no regard for existential *malaise*, the agonizing of philosophers over the question whether man signifies as something or as nothing in the universe. To care about being something was on a par with caring about becoming something: the same kind of preoccupation with the self. It is in the thought of the fragility, arbitrariness or unworthiness of the self that many of our problems arise, and it is upon such thinking that they thrive. But really to experience these states is a different matter. When Krishnamurti said 'be dead to love', 'be insensitive', 'be envious', 'be hateful', 'be nothing', he was not counselling self-acceptance, but a sustained awareness that would not allow itself to be diminished either by self-blame or self-satisfaction. It was this which would eventually dissolve not the problem but the maker of the problem, the proud and mischievously cunning self.

When our problems arise in the context of our relationships they may seem to be of a different kind from the problems that we have with ourselves, more complex because there are other selves involved, perhaps more urgent because they call for decision and action. Fundamentally though, they are not much different. They spring from the same conflict between the fact of 'what is' and the idea of what should be, and their resolution likewise depends upon watchfulness and awareness. We need relationship, life exists only in relationship, not to relate is to be dead, but relationship involves love. Although it is the received wisdom that love is the answer to every problem, in most people's experience love raises the most overwhelming problems of all. Finding it, keeping it, losing it, understanding it, evaluating its varieties – the sexual, the spiritual, the familial – give us no end of problems. Love liberates, takes us out of ourselves, but it also binds, and the self surrendered in passion often resents its bondage on reflection.

A young woman went to Krishnamurti to discuss her wish to be free from her husband, with whom she no longer had a physical relationship. She said she resented him and wanted nothing more to do with him. Krishnamurti said that so long as she resented him she was not free, asking why she resented him. She said she had found him to be mean, unloving and selfish, and the thought of having had anything to do with him made her feel unclean. 'I cannot tell you what horror I have discovered in him,' she said. Krishnamurti admonished her: 'He is what he is, so why be angry with him? Is your resentment really against him? Or, having seen what *is*, are you ashamed of yourself for having been associated with it?' He pursued the point until the woman admitted that it was so. She accepted that 'hate binds as love does', and that she would only be free from the relationship when she came to terms with the fact that it was really with herself that she was angry. But then she had another problem: how to be free from her shame, and how to wipe out the past, the memories of years that 'left a very bad taste in my mouth'. 'Why do you want to wipe it out?' Krishnamurti asked, suggesting that it may be because she had a certain idea and estimation of herself that those memories contradicted. Her fundamental problem was that she had 'put herself on a pedestal called self-esteem'. 'If you can understand this', he told her, 'then there will be no shame of the past; it will have completely gone. You will be what you are without the pedestal.'[3]

In the problems of relationship, although we may lay the blame upon the other, it is often still the imp of the self that is the mischief-maker. The self demands esteem, both in its own eyes and those of others. In its uncertainty and fragility it often acquiesces to pressure from others to conform to certain patterns of conduct that are regarded as the norm or the ideal – that pressure is particularly strong when it is endorsed by the society, the class, or the religion to which a person belongs. This was the problem of another young woman, also no longer in love with her husband, who had been violent with her, and was now living with her children apart from him. Should she go back to him? she asked. Of course, Krishnamurti would not answer the question, but he made her see that the reason she was confused was that she was worried about respectability, that her concern about what she ought to do was preventing her seeing clearly 'what is'. She imagined that she was in a situation of choice, but any choice she made in a state of confusion would only lead to further confusion. 'How am I to be clear about what I should do?' the woman asked, and Krishnamurti answered: 'Action does not follow clarity: clarity *is* action . . . If what *is* is clear, then you will see that there is no choice but only action.' The woman said she would try to be clear, without the persuasion of respectability or any calculation of self-interest, then asked, 'But what of love?' Krishnamurti said that from what she had told him it was clear that, like most people, she had used the word love, and had married, to make respectable things that really had nothing to do with it, like fear of insecurity, loneliness and the fulfilment of physical urges and needs. These things, and respectability, are determined by thought, and 'love is not thought . . . Love is not sensation . . . There can be no deliberate action for love, because love is not of the mind.'[3]

So what is love? Many of our problems of relationship arise from our misunderstanding or misusing the word, and from the ideas and expectations we have of love. Krishnamurti states and interrogates some common misconceptions:

> Is not jealousy an indication of love? We hold hands, and then the next minute scold; we say hard things, but soon embrace. We quarrel, then kiss and are reconciled. Is not all this love? The very expression of jealousy is an indication of love; they seem to go together like light and darkness. The swift anger and the caress – are these not the fullness of love? . . . What is it that we call love? It is the whole field of jealousy, of lust, of harsh words, of caresses, of holding hands, of quarrelling and making up. These are the facts in this field of so-called love . . . There is conflict, confusion and antagonism within this field which we call love. But is it love?[3]

No, he maintains, love is none of this. As darkness cannot exist where there is light, so jealousy and conflict cannot exist where there is love. Love is not something brought into existence by its object, and dependent for its continuity upon its object maintaining those attributes that evoked it. Those attributes are apprehended by the mind, they engender pleasure and desire, which thought dwells upon, and they constitute an object which the self, and *soi-disant* lover, seeks to possess. The conflicts and turbulences of what we call our love relationships are really conflicts of the self. Where love is, the self is not, so there is no possessiveness. Love, Krishnamurti often said, is a flame without smoke: it is the self, with its desires, expectations and insecurities, that generates the smoke which obscures and can stifle it.

A young woman told Krishnamurti that she was tortured by jealousy and wanted to be rid of it, but her love for her husband and children was such that she was unable to control her jealousy. 'Are you saying that love and jealousy go together?' he asked her. She said it seemed so. 'In that case,' Krishnamurti said, 'if you are free from jealousy you have also got rid of love, haven't you?' Her problem was that she wanted to keep the pleasure of attachment and be rid of the pain of it. What she should examine and be aware of, he said, were her fears, because attachment implies fear. The woman confessed a bundle of fears: of not being loved, of insecurity, loneliness, of something happening to the children or her husband, of his turning to another woman. She saw now, she said, that attachment and psychological dependence were not love, and that her jealousy had been based upon selfishness. And now, Krishnamurti said, she was condemning herself, which was another evasion of understanding. 'You have to understand the complex entity which is you,' he said, 'without condemning or justifying.' To name feelings, to speak of jealousy, selfishness, fear of loneliness, does not help understanding and awareness. Words are loaded with implications of condemnation or justification, and 'the verbalising process is part of the self'. Only 'when there is no naming. . .', then the mind does not separate itself from that which is.'[4]

Do we not too glibly speak of love? Do not many of our problems in our relationships arise because we deceive ourselves and others by taking the word for the thing itself? Is not love something that we bring into a relationship rather than something that we look to the relationship to bring out in ourselves and the other? Is it not, therefore, independent of its object, and consequently non-possessive? And when we seek it, try to hold on to it or lament losing it, are we not engaging it with aspects of the self and the mind that have nothing to do with it?

Yes, these are truths we can hardly contradict. But, we ask, what about sex? This is *the* big problem area in life for many people. The jealousies, the conflicts, the quarrels, the swift transitions from anger to caresses, the turbulences of passion that, as Krishnamurti oberved, are commonly believed to be the norm of love relationships, generally have their origin in sex. When we need to resolve problems that we have with our sexuality or in our sexual relationships, we will pay scant regard to any resolution that we feel does not take account of the strength and compulsiveness of sexuality in human life. Sex is a fact of our biology. We may acknowledge that other problems we have are of the mind, but sex is of the body, and we may wonder whether any problems we have with it are going to be resolved by non-judgemental passive awareness when the thing itself subverts and contradicts passivity. We may question, too, whether sex is a demand of the self, when we experience it as something self-annulling or self-transcending. Manifestly human beings are least regardful of self and self-interest when under its thrall.

So what did Krishnamurti have to say about sex, and was what he had to say based on an understanding of its compulsiveness? Here are some extracts from a reply he gave to a questioner who said, 'I am very seriously disturbed by the sex urge. How am I to overcome it?'

> Please bear with me if I do not tell you how to overcome the sex urge; but we are going to study the problem together, to see what is involved, and as we study the problem you will find the right answer for yourself. First, let us understand the problem of overcoming... That which can be overcome has to be overcome or conquered again and again... Whereas, if you understand something, it is over. So if there is a problem, as the questioner has, of sex, we must understand it and not merely ask: how can it be overcome?
>
> Because all our pleasures are mechanical, sex has become the only pleasure which is creative... Emotionally we are machines carrying out a routine, and the machine is not creative... So, as we are hedged all-round by the uncreative thinking, there is only one thing left to us, and that is sex. As sex is the only thing that is left it becomes an enormous problem, whereas if we understood what it means to be creative religiously and emotionally, to be creative at all moments... surely then sex would become an insignificant problem...
>
> A man who has real love in his heart has no sorrow and to him sex is not a problem. But since we have lost love, sex has become a great problem and a different one because we are caught in it, by habit, by imagination and by yesterday's memory which threatens us and binds us... Most of the time we are enclosed in our own cravings, wants and fears, and naturally the only outlet is sex, which degenerates, enervates and becomes a problem. So, while looking at this problem, we begin to discover our own state, that is what *is*; not how to transform it, but how to be aware of it. Do not condemn it, do not try to sublimate it or find substitutions, or overcome it. Simply be aware of it, of all it means.[38]

Most of the people who discussed with Krishnamurti the problems they had with sex were conditioned to regard it negatively, as subversive of the spiritual life. But he did not so regard it. A young couple in India who were married but had vowed, because they were 'very religiously inclined', not to have a sexual relationship, and were now tormented by frustration, were asked:

> Is it a religious life to punish yourself? Is mortification of the body or of the mind a sign of understanding? Is self-torture a way to reality? Do you think you can go far through renunciation? Passion has to be understood, not suppressed or sublimated. How can you love and understand passion if you have taken a vow against it? A vow is a form of resistance, and what you resist ultimately conquers you.[4]

Krishnamurti was appalled by the violence that some sannyasis in

India perpetrated upon themselves in trying to overcome their sexuality, for it not only failed in its object but also rendered them insensitive to the marvels and beauty of the world, life and nature. Sex is only a problem if we make it one, by seeking or rejecting it for the wrong reasons. In fact, any reasons will be wrong, because they are of the mind. 'Is sex the product of thought?' Krishnamurti asked:

> Is sex – the pleasure, the delight, the companionship, the tenderness involved in it – is this a remembrance strengthened by thought? In the sexual act there is self-forgetfulness, self-abandonment, a sense of the non-existence of fear, anxiety, the worries of life. Remembering this state of tenderness and self-forgetfulness, and demanding its repetition, you chew over it, as it were, until the next occasion. Is this tenderness, or is it merely a recollection of something that is over and which, through repetition, you hope to capture again? Is not the repetition of something, however pleasurable, a destructive process?[8]

We acknowledge that sexual desire exists prior to and independent of the object that focuses it, because it is biological and therefore natural. If we do not so readily acknowledge that the same applies to love, the implication is that love is not natural in the same sense, and we are into problems with ideas about the lower and higher, baser and nobler, attributes of human nature. Sex as an expression or action of love is not problematical, we only have problems when sex and love don't coexist, when the mind separates them, by evaluating, or by seeking the one through the other. To masquerade love in order to get sex, or to engage in sex to secure the imagined satisfactions of love – security, tenderness, or whatever – are actions guaranteed to give rise to problems. Krishnamurti's basic principles apply to the sexual as to any other problems in life: they will only be resolved by watchful vigilance, passive awareness and the clear understanding of 'what is', which includes the understanding that basically, 'you are the problem'.

The word 'problem', Krishnamurti often pointed out, in its Greek derivation, originally meant 'something thrown at you'. He wanted to make the point that when something is thrown at you, you only have two options, to catch it or to dodge it, and the decision and the action are simultaneous – 'the decision acts'. The definition also serves to specify another kind of problem, seemingly different from those we have with ourselves or our relationships, that is, the problems that arise from situations that life throws at us, the misfortunes, losses, reversals and tragedies that afflict human life and for which we are manifestly blameless. Religions have formulaic solaces for the misfortunes that life visits upon us: they are the will of God, the expiation of bad karma carried over from a previous life, things 'sent to try us'. If they seem unjust we may be assured that there will be an ultimate balancing of accounts, on Judgement Day or in a future incarnation. Krishnamurti, of course, could offer no such consolations, and when people discussed their personal tragedies with him they were sometimes shocked by his response.

A woman who had lost her husband and one of her children visited Krishnamurti in the company of her uncle, a devout Hindu. The uncle said that none of the ceremonies or beliefs of their religion had been able to console the woman, and indeed when she told her story she wept copiously all the time. When she had finished, Krishnamurti asked her if she had come to him because she wanted to talk about death and bereavement seriously or in order to be comforted by some explanation, to be distracted from her grief by some reassuring words. She said that she wanted to go into the subject deeply, though she didn't know if she would be able to face what he was going to say to her.

He asked her to examine her sorrow, and to ask whether it was for her husband or for herself. 'If you are crying for him,' he said,

> can your tears help him? He has gone irrevocably. Do what you will, you will never have him back. But if you are crying for yourself, because of your loneliness, your empty life, because of the sensual pleasures you had and the companionship, then you are crying, aren't you, out of your own emptiness and out of self-pity? . . . Now that he has gone you are realising, aren't you, your own actual state? His death has shaken you and shown you the actual state of your mind and heart. You may not be willing to look at it; you may reject it out of fear, but if you observe a little more you will see that you are crying out of your own loneliness, out of your inward poverty – which is, out of self-pity.

This was cruel, the woman said, and there was no comfort in it for her. Krishnamurti replied that comfort was always based on illusion, that the only way to go beyond sorrow was to see things as they really were, and that surely it was not cruelty to point this out. Death was inevitable for everyone, and 'one has to come in touch with this enormous fact of life'. At this point the uncle protested that there is in everyone an immortal soul which goes through a series of incarnations until it achieves perfection. Krishnamurti replied: 'There is nothing permanent either on earth or in ourselves', and explained how thought and memory create the illusion of permanence as a refuge from fear of the unknown. Returning to the woman's situation, he urged her to concern herself with the upbringing of her remaining three children instead of with her own misery and self-pity. If she saw the absurdity of these feelings, he said, 'then you will naturally stop crying, stop isolating yourself, and live with the children with a new light and with a smile on your face'.[9]

Krishnamurti knew the grief of bereavement, for in 1925 he had lost his brother Nitya and for a time had been inconsolable. He was always compassionate with those who grieved, but he was unsparing with the feelings of the aggrieved. A man whose son had died in an accident and whose wife had left him told Krishnamurti that in his experience it was not true that wisdom comes through suffering. He had suffered a great deal in life and had found quite the contrary. To the question, 'What has sorrow taught you?' he answered that he had learnt not to be attached, to keep aloof, control his feelings and take care not to get hurt again. Krishnamurti said: 'So, as you say, it hasn't taught you wisdom; on the contrary, it has made you more cunning, more insensitive. Does sorrow teach one anything at all except self-protective reactions?'[10] In sorrow, he added, there was always self-pity, and where there was self-pity there could never be understanding.

A couple in India who had a blind child asked Krishnamurti what they could have done, in this life or a previous one, to deserve this punishment. He said bluntly that the child's blindness probably had a physical or genetic cause and asked them why they sought a metaphysical one. The man answered that by knowing the cause he would better understand the effect. 'You mean that you will take comfort in knowing how this thing has come about, do you not?' said Krishnamurti. The man said it would certainly be comforting. Krishnamurti said, 'Then you want comfort and not understanding', and to the man's question whether they were not the same thing, he answered: 'Understanding a fact may cause disturbance, it does not necessarily bring joy . . . You are disturbed by the fact of your son's ailment, and you want to be pacified.' The man protested: 'Why shouldn't one seek freedom from disturbance? Why shouldn't one avoid suffering?' Krishnamurti replied:

> Through avoidance is there freedom from suffering? To avoid suffering is only to strengthen it. The explanation of the cause is not the

understanding of the cause. Through explanation you are not freed from suffering; the suffering is still there, only you have covered it over with words.[3]

Far from dispensing consolations and pacifiers, Krishnamurti often gave the disturbed deeper cause for disturbance. A prominent politician's wife, who said she was sick with anxiety after months of nursing her husband, whose illness the doctors said was fatal, wept and told Krishnamurti that she couldn't bear to lose him and see everything they had lived and worked for falling apart. He asked her, 'Do you love your husband or do you love the things which came about through him?' When she couldn't answer he begged her not to think the question brutal, for she would eventually have to uncover the truth of it, 'otherwise sorrow will always be there'. The woman went away saying that at present she was too confused and distressed to think, but she returned several months later, after her husband had died, saying that now she could look at things more clearly. 'Your question disturbed me more than I can tell you,' she said, and coming back to it she said, 'Love is a mixture of so many things.' Krishnamurti dismissed her evasion and pressed her to confront the truth, whereupon she admitted – saying that she was appalled at herself for doing so – that she hadn't loved her husband at all.[4]

The truth, the fact of *what is*, may hurt, but then the hurt too becomes a part of *what is*, enters the flux that is always and simultaneously an ending and a new beginning. Only the hurt avoided endures – only the lie unacknowledged, the explanation grasped for solace, the word masquerading as the thing, the solution found by thought, kill awareness and make our problems endure. Maybe secretly we want them to endure, because we cannot imagine what we would be or life would be without them. That is our choice, but it's a choice of unfreedom. Krishnamurti did not offer any answers, but he did, lucidly and unequivocally, show us the alternative.

15

Science and the Future: the Bohm Dialogues

KRISHNAMURTI'S statements that there is no path to truth, that the thought-activity of the brain is ultimately futile and irrelevant, and that problems are not things to be solved but just observed, would provoke in many a scientist the derision of one whose very *raison d'être* has been called in question. Has not science proved the most staggeringly successful truth-seeking activity of man, and does it not owe its great achievements to rational thought and a methodology based on problem-solving? Either Krishnamurti must have used words with different connotations than those that scientists accord them, or his statements must be seen as reinforcing the widely believed-in incompatibility of the religious and the scientific views of life and the world.

Certainly unquestioning faith, idolatry, and the resolution of spiritual and metaphysical perplexity in the doctrinaire fixation of belief, are incompatible with the inquiring and empirical spirit of science. But these are the very characteristics of religions that Krishnamurti rejected. 'A religious mind,' he said, 'is a very factual mind; it deals with facts, with what is actually happening with the world outside and the world inside.'[20] On the basis of this definition, the religious and scientific minds should not be incompatible, but on the contrary they should be capable of dialogue and cross-fertilization. The obstacles to dialogue have not all been one-sided, however. Scientists themselves are not unsusceptible to the appeal of a dogma which settles the question of what is real or relevant and furnishes a ground for getting on with their experimental and theoretical projects. The view that there is only a material reality, and that everything in the universe can be comprehended in terms of the mechanics of that reality, is that dogma. It is as much scientists' adherence to it as the religious mind's adherence to its belief in the primacy of a spiritual reality that has prevented much significant dialogue. But increasingly throughout the present century the materialistic-mechanistic bias of physical science has been subverted by experiment and theory, particularly in the area of quantum physics. Indeed many of the acknowledged greatest contributors to this area of science, such as Niels Bohr, Wolfgang Pauli and Werner Heisenberg, have made statements and developed theories akin to those of the mystical and metaphysical philosophies that formerly derived from the supposedly pre-scientific world- and life-view. In these circumstances, with the loosening of the fetters of dogma and doctrinaire bias on both sides, dialogue has become possible.

Dr David Bohm is a distinguished theoretical physicist who has held professorships at universities in the United States, England and Israel, and is the author of several textbooks on quantum physics. He started having dialogues with Krishnamurti in the early 1970s, bringing to them a mind aware of both the demands and the limitations of scientific reasoning. Bohm is aware also, as a quantum physicist, of the ambiguities, indeterminacies and seemingly unfathomable mysteries which dispose the mind that seeks to comprehend the ultimate secrets of physical reality towards a view which encompasses mental and spiritual factors as inalienable components of that reality. Bohm's own book, *Wholeness and the Implicate Order*, is in many respects a development and extension of the Krishnamurti philosophy within the context of scientific theory – and I discuss it as such in the Appendix. It is not a matter of influence, however, but of two minds of very different backgrounds and complexions converging with and cross-fertilizing each other.

It is natural that Krishnamurti, with his aversion to being regarded as an authority or guru, should have preferred to engage in dialogue rather than address an audience. Indeed, when he was talking to a large audience he often tried to create the atmosphere of an intimate dialogue, saying for instance: 'As a matter of fact there is only you and I talking together. . ., sitting on the banks of a river, on a bench, talking over this thing.'[20] Good dialogue is a living process in which meaning emerges from the flow and exchange of ideas. It is a process of inquiry and clarification, of 'finding out'. Through interaction, meanings emerge that would otherwise have remained unexpressed. Good dialogue is not debate, not intellectual sparring, it is a meeting of minds, endowed with experience and information but divested of bias, concerned to disclose truth and meaning through their interaction.

This is what happens in the Krishnamurti-Bohm dialogues. The thirteen dialogues published in the volume *The Ending of Time* took place between April and September 1980. They range widely and constitute a quite comprehensive summing up of the teaching and, furthermore, developments and explications of Krishnamurti's thought emerge in them that are not so clearly expressed in any other context. What we have in these dialogues is an ongoing thought process in which two minds participate, exploring a familiar territory of discourse in full awareness of the limitations of the method of exploration, which nevertheless yields insights and meanings that would otherwise not be disclosed.

The term 'insight', in fact, is a central one in the dialogues, where it is invested with a meaning more akin to 'an illumination' than 'an *aperçu*'. Insight, Krishnamurti says, is generated by intelligence, as distinct from thought which generates knowledge. It is a function not of the brain but of the Mind – the capital 'M' signifying the universal as distinct from the particular. Insight is endowed with energy. It may come 'in a flash' but it is not ephemeral like a lightning flash. It is possessed of an energy that sustains itself, and furthermore that can act upon the physical structure of the brain to effect a radical change in it. Free of the energy-draining activities of thought, insight is the only thing that can galvanize change in the individual and the world. But it is not something that anyone can give us, or that we can get for ourselves by any amount or kind of effort. To whoever has it, it seems a perfectly natural thing, but he may be perplexed to find few, if any, others so endowed: there is nothing much he can do to help except 'bring light'.

Krishnamurti rarely talked about himself, and would only do so occasionally with his closest friends. He does so here, and one of the chief interests of the dialogues lies in the self-revelations they contain, and in the way he and Bohm together explore their implications. A key passage occurs early in the first dialogue:

> K: One night in India I woke up; it was a quarter past twelve, I looked at the watch. And – I hesitate to say this because it sounds extravagant – the source of all energy had been reached. And that had an extraordinary effect on the brain. And also physically. I'm sorry to talk about myself, but, you understand, literally, there was no division at all; no sense of the world, of 'me'. You follow? Only this sense of a tremendous source of energy.

DB: So the brain was in contact with this source of energy?

K: Yes, and as I have been talking for sixty years, I would like others to reach this – no, not *reach* it. You understand what I am saying? All our problems are solved. Because it is pure energy from the very beginning of time. Now how am I – not 'I', you understand – how is one not to teach, not to help, or push, – but how is one to say, 'This way leads to a complete sense of peace, of love'? I am sorry to use all these words. But suppose you have come to that point and your brain itself is throbbing with it – how would you help another to come to that?

Krishnamurti's conviction that the experience he talks about here involved an actual change in the physical structure of his brain, and his further belief that it is possible for others to undergo such a change, is a recurrent theme in the dialogues. Such a change in the brain cannot be construed in terms of 'becoming', as something which takes place in time, so when the discussion turns to evolution, Krishnamurti says the theory seem to him 'totally untrue psychologically'. Bohm points out that the evidence for the evolution of the brain as a physical entity is irrefutable, proposing the clarification that the brain has evolved in time but the mind has not, furthermore that time has become a part of the very structure of the brain. Krishnamurti agrees, adding that both thought and knowledge are time-binding functions of the brain, and that a brain thus bound can never experience true freedom or insight. 'Time is the enemy,' he declares. 'Meet it, and go beyond it.'

How did this entrapment in time occur? Did the human species at some point in its evolution take 'a wrong turn'? These are the questions with which Krishnamurti opens the first dialogue. They agree that something of the kind must have happened. Bohm contributes the observation that he had read somewhere that man 'went wrong' some five or six thousand years ago, when he began plundering and taking slaves. They agree further that this 'taking a wrong turn' was not only an evolutionary aberration, but is something that we continue to do all the time because we are governed by patterns of thought and behaviour laid down in the past, be they instinctual or formed by experience and its resultant 'knowledge', which shut off the possibilities of insight and change. These patterns are tenacious because one of man's fundamental instincts is for security, and he thinks that he will only find security in the realm of the known. He balks at change because it is entry into the unknown, but most of all he balks at relinquishing his time-bound condition because his sense of personal identity is constituted by it. He has a sense of having become what he is, and having acquired, in time, the knowledge that he has, which he values as consolidating his sense of self. He believes that this process will continue, that in time and through the accumulation of more knowledge and experience he may become better or more highly developed. So he continues to take 'the wrong turning', not realizing that the basic problem is his ego-consciousness. His sense of self, and wish to enhance or develop that spurious entity, is not only a prison in which he is entrapped but also the root cause of divisiveness in the world. It is this which from time immemorial has set man against man and nation against nation, giving rise to a general barbarism and destructive energy that threatens the very survival of the human species, making a mockery of any ameliorative project, whether of the individual in respect of his own life, or of the collective in the form of religious or political movements. These movements have not only failed to better mankind and the world but now bid fair to be the very agents of their destruction.

I summarize the gist of several discussions. And briefly to digress, I think it relevant to draw attention to the fact that the idea of man having taken a wrong turn in the process of evolution has been expressed by others, notably Dr Julian Jaynes and Arthur Koestler, with interesting correspondences with Krishnamurti's views. Jaynes. in his book *The Origin of Consciousness in the Breakdown of the Bicameral Mind*, maintains that ancient man (of about five to six thousand years ago – this is probably the theory that Bohm was alluding to) possessed no self-consciousness or subjectivity, 'no awareness of his awareness of the world, no internal mind space to introspect upon',[43] and that it was with and through the emergence of self-awareness that wilful cruelty and murderous violence became intrinsic characteristics of human behaviour. Arthur Koestler, too, maintained that 'something went wrong' in the evolution of *homo sapiens*, going so far as to say that we 'may be an aberrant biological species, afflicted by an endemic disorder . . . a flaw, some potentially fatal engineering error built into the circuits of our nervous system.' The neocortex and the hypothalamus, the new brain and the old, he suggested, are out of synchrony, and this dichotomy may explain 'the chronic conflict between rational thought and irrational beliefs, the resulting paranoid streak in our history, the contrast between the growth-curves of science and ethics.'[44] The only remedy that Koestler could propose for 'evolution's glaring mistake' was the development of some chemical corrective to the old brain's dominance. On this point Krishnamurti would have disagreed with him. But the interesting correspondence is that both maintained that the human brain must change, otherwise man is doomed.

Can it change? Will it? And how can it? These are the pivotal questions in the dialogues. Having taken a wrong turn in the past, can man now take a right turn? Yes, Krishnamurti answers. If I have being going North all my life and I suddenly realize that going North means everlasting conflict, I can stop, and start going East. It is entirely rational, and basically simple, whereas it is totally irrational, in the light of history, to believe that change can be accomplished gradually, in time and through effort. He asks why people don't see the fallacy and irrationality of this belief. Bohm answers that they may see it when it is pointed out, but the principle of achieving through effort and struggle is so deeply ingrained in human thought and behaviour, so intrinsic a part of the patterning, that it cannot so easily be broken down. Normally it takes something really big, by way of a crisis, to break a behavioural pattern, and even then there is a tendency subsequently to fall back into the old ways.

Part of the problem is that the mind tends to turn everything into an idea, into knowledge, which is a kind of defensive mechanism against radical change. We may know that something is wrong, but that mere knowledge does not generate the energy to change the wrong. As Krishnamurti puts it, 'all the fuel is there, but the fire is not'. Knowledge, in fact, positively inhibits change. We think of knowledge as something just sitting there, available for our use, says Bohm, whereas in fact it is extremely active, 'meeting and shaping every moment according to past knowledge', and turning everything into thought and ideas. A distinction has to be made, they agree, between knowledge for instance of a language, a skill or a specific subject, such as science, which has its use, and conceptual and psychological knowledge, which masquerades as similarly useful but really serves no purpose except to keep the mind stuck in its time-bound rut, resistant to novelty and change. Krishnamurti goes further, maintaining that such knowledge actually 'withers the brain', saps and dissipates its energy and makes it dull, petty in its concerns and incapable of attention.

Attention, in fact, Krishnamurti proposes, may be the very factor necessary to bring about change. Not attention in the sense of concentration or mind-focusing, and certainly not in the manner advocated by teachers of meditation techniques. It is not a matter of 'paying attention', for instance to a problem. In fact, 'where there is attention there is no problem', because there is no thought, and above all 'no centre from which "I" attend'. The inattentive mind languishes in a state of 'indolence, negligence, self-concern, self-contradiction'; its operations are confused and fragmented and it tends to identify itself with many other things. The attentive mind, by contrast, entertains no sense of self, it is empty of thought and knowledge, but it is imbued with tremendous energy, which sustains its capacity to attend. Whereas the inattentive mind is in a state of perpetual disorder and tends to look outside itself for ordering principles – to authorities, gurus, religions and suchlike – the attentive mind is intrinsically orderly: when it looks outside itself it does so with total clarity and rationality, apprehending 'what is'.

Some elucidations are called for here, and Bohm draws them out. The distinction has been made between the physical brain, the individual or particular mind that interacts with it, and the universal Mind. Krishnamurti has said that when the mind gets rid of its time-binding content of thought and knowledge it ceases to exist in its particularity and merges with Mind. Then the energetic interaction of Mind with the brain, which hitherto has been blocked by the operations of the individual mind, brings about a change in the physical structure of the brain, an actual mutation and renewal of the brain cells. So Krishnamurti argues, but Bohm points out that scientists would be sceptical about the possibility of a renewal of the brain cells, and also that it does not follow logically that a brain that is not time-bound will regenerate. Krishnamurti replies, 'I think they can be renewed', and says he thinks that it does follow logically because that brain is no longer of an individual, but is universal, so it has tremendous energy. The problem with the individual brain-mind is that it consumes its energy with internal conflicts, but as soon as those conflicts end what is left is pure Mind and energy, and it is not illogical to say that this energy might change the physical structure of the brain. What brings about the ending of conflict is insight, and sustained insight is attention. With the energy of insight and attention the brain can change, Krishnamurti maintains, and he asks Bohm what science would have to say about that.

Bohm answers that materialistic science would have very little to say. Krishnamurti's statements imply that insight is something beyond the brain which can effect a change in it, which further implies that something non-material can affect matter. It is clear and agreed that the processes of thought cannot effect a physical change, but what is not clear is whether it is effected by something other than the brain or by something deeper *in* the brain. The question is whether there is a function of the brain that is independent of and not conditioned by its content, but is still a physical function. Krishnamurti sees a danger in this approach, in that it might be construed as implying that 'there is God in me'. But Bohm pursues it, proposing that there could be a natural activity of the brain that could awaken somehow, and change it. To Krishnamurti's question whether this would still be a material action, he replies that there could be different levels of matter, and a deeper level in the brain unconditioned by thought. Thought, Krishnamurti asserts, is matter. Bohm demurs, suggesting the qualification that it is a process in matter, analogous to waves, which are a movement or process in matter but not themselves material. But this distinction begs the question, merely reformulating it as: can a material process in the brain bring about a change in itself, or is there another activity which is not a material process? Krishnamurti proposes that insight is independent of the material process, but yet can act upon it. Bohm points out that in the physical world as scientists observe it, one-sided action never occurs, there is always reciprocity, although philosophically its possibility has been proposed, for instance in the Aristotelian concept of God as the 'Unmoved Mover'. 'Would you say that Aristotle had insight?' Krishnamurti asks mischievously, and Bohm replies in kind: 'he said some things that suggest he was quite intelligent, at least.'

The touch of levity is appropriate because the basic question cannot be resolved in the terms of the discussion, in which Bohm has been, for argument's sake, representing the view of orthodox science, although in fact he is more in accord with Krishnamurti's view. He now sums up this view, asking: 'Are we saying that insight is an energy which illuminates the activity of the brain? And that in this illumination, the brain itself begins to act differently?' To which Krishnamurti replies: 'You are quite right. That's all. That is what takes place. Yes.' When they return to the point in a later discussion, Bohm brings in the analogy of sudden cancer remissions, which are inexplicable to medical science, and suggests that insight might bring about a corresponding change in the brain cells, dismantling wrong neuronal connections and establishing a new order, or rather bringing order where there was formerly disorder.

Whenever God comes into the discussions, Krishnamurti's tendency is to despatch Him promptly, either with a quip or a shrug. God as a concept, an idea or ideal, he considers, has been responsible for too much of mankind's misdirected activity. But when he and Bohm speak of 'the ground', as they frequently do, the discussion enters upon distinctly theological territory. Bohm introduces the term early in the dialogues. They have talked about the universal Mind, and Krishnamurti says that beyond that there is something more of which it is a part. Bohm says, 'Could we say that this something more is the ground of the whole?' Picking up from what Krishnamurti had said a little earlier about the experience he had woken up to in India, and perhaps relating it to the discoveries that have been made in his own field of quantum physics, he further proposes that 'the ground of everything is energy'. Krishnamurti agrees, adding that 'energy exists only when there is emptiness', but then he appears to retract his agreement, saying: 'There is something in us that is operating, there is something in us much more – much – I don't know how to put it – much greater. What I'm trying to say is, I think there is something beyond that.' 'Beyond the emptiness, the ground of the emptiness?' Bohm asks, and pursues the logic that this something must necessarily be different from emptiness, and therefore presumably must have substance. But Krishnamurti balks at the idea of substance, or of attributing any qualities to the 'something beyond', saying that the mind cannot grasp, comprehend, or even look at it. Bohm argues that logically this regression can go on, that the existence of a something beyond the 'something' can be posited, although Krishnamurti says categorically, 'There is nothing beyond it. I stick to that. I feel that is the beginning and ending of everything.' Bohm clarifies this, in terms of 'the ground' being that from which everything comes and to which everyting returns, the universal as well as the particular. Krishnamurti agrees, adding: 'Everything is dying, except *that*.'

Krishnamurti's tentativeness on the one hand, and his expressions of conviction on the other, in these discussions of 'the ground', relieve their abstractness and persuade us that they are talking about something meaningful to him personally and related to his experience. The abstractness worries him. 'Does that convey anything?' he asks, after making the above statement, and later: 'Is the ground an idea, imagination, illusion, a philosophic concept?' Merely talking about it, coolly and abstractly, without passion, is pointless. The question is: 'What has that to do with man? ... There must be a connection. There must be some relationship with the ground ... Otherwise, what is the meaning of living?'

The meaning to religious people, Bohm replies, is that 'the ground' is not indifferent to mankind. But how can we find out if this is true? Krishnamurti asks. We cannot get at it by way of thought or knowledge, because '*that* is not knowledge, it is not something that can be put together or perceived by thought'. Can science get at it? Is the scientist, when he investigates the real nature of matter, trying to find 'the ground'? Yes, he is, Bohm answers, 'that's exactly it, precisely, yes', expressing, however, more his personal conviction than that of scientists in general, because as he later observes: 'You might think that if they saw the whole unity of the universe they would act differently, but they don't.' Science, he admits, with its reductionist methodology, has divested the universe of meaning, analysing physical and material processes as things 'just going on', and this has prevailed over the old religious view that existence is given meaning by something beyond the material.

But didn't the religious people merely invent meaning? Krishnamurti asks, and again: 'How would one discover, or find out, or touch it — if the ground exists at all?' — without the investigation being prejudiced by the feeling that if it doesn't exist human life has no meaning. There is a way, he suggests, and that is by meeting the demands of 'the ground', which are for 'absolute silence, absolute emptiness ... no sense of egotism in any form'. He adds a cautionary point: when religious people say that you can't find it by being rational, it doesn't mean that you can by being irrational, because 'the ground' is '*the* most rational', and to reach it we must 'find the cause of irrationality [in ourselves] and wipe it out'. The fundamental cause is the supreme importance that man has given to thought, which 'being limited, divisive, incomplete, can never be rational'. Rationality is based on awareness, seeing, watching and recognizing 'what is', and the first essential is that we be aware of and recognize the roots and workings of irrationality in our own lives. Then, 'if we are completely rational, there is total insight.' By way of clarifying this, Bohm suggests that they make a distinction between 'rationality of thought', which is the everongoing, memory-governed, mechanical process of the brain, and 'rationality of perception'. Krishnamurti agrees that it is the latter that leads to 'instant insight, which is not of time, which is not of memory, which has no cause'.

Through insight, then, and in people endowed with insight, 'the ground' becomes manifest. Krishnamurti expresses a conviction that if ten people could do it, could meet the demands of 'the ground', then it would demonstrably be there, and any scientist would accept it as a real fact, not something based on belief or illusion. But, he says ruefully, there are not ten people.

There are countless people who aspire to insight, and who want a relationship to 'the ground', and Krishnamurti can identify with them and articulate their dilemma. 'What shall I do,' he asks, 'if I vaguely see that coming upon this ground gives immense significance to life,' and as an educated, thoughtful man I reject the approaches of the religions because I see they are based on 'illusion created by desire, hope and fear'. I may intellectually understand the statement that thought is limited and must end, 'but I have no feeling for it; there is no perfume in it.' I may put to myself the fundamental question, which is, 'why do I always live in this centre of "me"?' and I may 'want to have this passion that will explode me out of this little enclosure'. But wanting is part of the problem: 'This petty little thing wants to have a relationship with that immensity. It cannot.' I may 'have shed tears, left my family, *everything* for that. And *that* says "No relationship".' The shock of this rejection, and the realization of the futility of all that I have done and thought, may create the emptiness that is the prerequisite of insight, but for this to happen I have to 'receive the full blow of it' and not cushion the shock by turning it into a concept or idea, which is to return to the familiar treadmill of thought and knowledge.

If he who aspires to relate to 'the ground' and to have insight asks, 'What shall I do?', so also does he in whom that insight and relationship are manifest. 'Suppose you have come to that point and your brain itself is throbbing with it – how would you help another?', Krishnamurti asked in the first dialogue, after talking about his own experience of having reached 'the source of all energy'. Later he is not so explicitly personal, preferring to speak of a fictitious 'X', who stands on the opposite side of a river bank to the aspirant 'Y', and to the latter's question, 'What shall I do?' can only answer, 'Cross'. If 'Y' asks how to cross, or wants first to be assured that there really is 'something beyond' that he can reach, 'X' can only reply, 'Explanations have been the boat in which to cross to the other shore ... But there is no boat'. When all he can say to help is simply 'Cross!', 'he is asking something impossible, isn't he?' There would appear to be an impasse, but, Bohm says,

'X' can have an effect upon 'Y', just by communicating the 'necessity of not going on with the old pattern, because you see it absolutely can't work'. Yes, Krishnamurti says, if 'Y' really listens to 'X', if he acknowledges that he is living in darkness and division, and instead of trying to move out of the darkness or heal the division he just listens; and if 'X' makes a statement that seems to him absolutely true, then that statement might enter into him and dispel the darkness instantly. There has been an effect in which explanations and the understanding of explanations have played no part; simply, 'X' has 'brought light'.

Krishnamurti brings up a question that he also discussed with his biographer Mary Lutyens (see p. 51): are people like 'X' freaks, human beings so unusual and uncommon that they might be rated unnatural? Bohm suggests that many people would say that. Krishnamurti replies, 'It goes against one's grain; I would not accept that.' Nor does he accept the view, common to the religions of the world, that 'the manifestation of the highest takes place occasionally'. 'X' is not an aberration, or an avatar or Messiah, and his insight is not some rare privilege miraculously bestowed. He and it are entirely natural, he maintains. So why are they so unusual? The answer must be, as already discussed, that man took and goes on taking 'the wrong turning'. Even if he doesn't turn away from 'X' as an unnatural being, but rather turns to him as an exemplar of the right way, or worships what he sees manifest in him, this is not going to enable him to make the radical change necessary to 'stop going North and start going East'.

So what is 'X's' function as a man in the world? What can he do, and what can be the effect of whatever he does? He may write, he may teach, he may heal, says Krishnamurti, but all those activities are rather 'trivial', they reduce 'X' to a function dictated by 'Y's' expectations as to how he may be helped, whereas 'X' has 'something much more than that, something immense'. The question is, 'how is that immensity operating on "Y"? . . . "X" is not satisfied with merely preaching and talking; that immensity which he is must have an effect, must do something.' Bohm asks, 'Why must it?', and Krishnamurti answers, 'Because light must affect darkness.' Interpreting this more specifically, Bohm asks if he is saying 'that somehow "X" makes possible an activity of the ground in the whole consciousness of mankind which would not have been possible without him'. Yes, Krishnamurti says, and compared to this all his talking, writing, and so on, are insignificant. Then Bohm puts a question that in another context and formulation was a pharasaic trap: 'Why does the ground require this man to operate on mankind?' Krishnamurti answers: 'It is part of existence, likes the stars ... The ground doesn't need the man, but the man has touched the ground, so the ground is using him, let's say employing him; he is part of that movement.' And as part of that movement, 'X' doesn't have to do anything specific, certainly not anything purposeful or conceived in terms of the results it might yield. It is 'Y' who thinks in terms of purposes and results, and who looks to 'X' for words or actions that will help him or will accomplish something. As Krishnamurti sums up the situation:

> You see man, 'Y', is concerned with concepts like 'show me', 'prove it to me', 'what benefit has it?', 'will it affect my future?' ... And he is looking at 'X' with eyes that are accustomed to this pettiness. So, he reduces that immensity to his pettiness, and puts it in a temple and has therefore lost it completely. But 'X' says, I won't even look at that; there is something so immense, please do look at it. 'X' brings light. That's all he can do. Isn't that enough?

Aware of the anthropomorphizing implications of speaking of 'the ground' using or employing 'X', Krishnamurti added, 'he is part of that movement.' 'Movement' is another key term in the dialogues, and requires some explanation. There are different kinds of movement. On the one hand, thought and the activities of the brain are characterized by movement, but this is a mechanical movement or material process of action and reaction. When that process stops, when the mind, no longer time-bound and thought-bound, becomes empty, it becomes at the same time suffused with a tremendous energy; so although it is still, in the sense of not being perturbed by the mechanical and reactive movements that formerly occupied it, there issues from that stillness a new kind of movement. This, Krishnamurti proposes, is the movement of creation, though not in the sense of the term as it is generally applied to the activities of artists or poets, whose creations are on the whole the products of skill, thought and knowledge, but creation in the sense of the issuing forth of the eternally new. The free and empty mind is creative in this sense; there is an unceasing movement out of its stillness which, because it is no longer a limited and particular mind, is part of the universal process of creation, of the order and activity of 'the ground' itself. This still but energetically active mind is in a state of meditation, and by extension it may be said that 'the universe, the cosmic order, is in meditation'. And because 'X' is a part of that movement, merely his being in the world must have an effect, there must emanate from him something not so specific as teachings or writings, something capable of catalyzing radical change.

'Bringing light' and emanating this influential 'something', may be the most effective things that 'X' can do in the world, but thus to state his function does rather remove him from the plane of human life and cares. In fact he is not removed in the sense of being indifferent or dismissive – perhaps only in the sense of being able to see and put these cares in a different perspective. He could not be indifferent because he embodies compassion and love, which are things that only come into being in their true nature and full force in one who is without ego. 'Compassion,' says Krishnamurti, 'is not "I am compassionate". It is not a feeling. Compassion is there, is something that is not "me".' Likewise love, and intelligence: the three go together, inseparably, and he in whom they are manifest is extraordinarily sensitive to human grief and sorrow, though he does not accept them as an inevitable part of the human condition. Seeing that they arise in and are sustained by a sense of individuality that is false, his compassion is not expressed in a sympathy that indulges the individual's concern with 'my grief' or 'my pain', but in seeking to awaken or convey the perception that suffering is rooted in thought and egocentricity; and only through the dissolution of the ego and the arising of the awareness that 'the world is me, and I am the world', will it end.

But do we human beings really want an end to sorrow and suffering? Bohm puts the question in a later dialogue.* He points out that people believe that they learn and grow through suffering, that it is precisely suffering that refines, purifies and ultimately dissolves the ego. This is a fallacy, Krishnamurti replies, because man obviously hasn't grown or changed through millennia of suffering. He has become no less egocentric, and the world he inhabits and creates has become no less violent and divided within and against itself. In fact, the pursuit of growth and change is the core problem. We can lay down and carry out plans and projects for cultivating a desert or building a bridge, but we cannot set about self-improvement in the same manner. 'Self-improvement,' says Krishnamurti, 'is something so utterly ugly.' The human psyche is what it is, and to conceive of it as potentially something other is merely an operation of thought, as is any attempt we

---

* See Bibliography, No. 23. The volume comprises two dialogues which took place in June 1983.

might make to accomplish that ideal. For instance, 'Human beings are violent. And they have been talking a great deal – Tolstoy, and in India – of non-violence. The fact is, we are violent. And the non-violence is not real.'[23] The two states cannot coexist in the psyche, and we delude ourselves if we think that by effort we can make a transition from the one to the other. All we can do is remain in and with our violence, not in the sense of accepting or exonerating it as 'only human', but observing it and its workings attentively, so that in that attention there might arise the perception that ends it.

Throughout these last dialogues, as throughout Krishnamurti's last talks, there runs the theme that to be complacent about the human condition or to acquiesce in the view that ameliorative projects can alleviate its distresses, could be an error more grave in its consequences than just perpetuating the individual suffering and existential *Angst* that for millennia the religions of the world have inadequately ministered to. There is not only the threat that man will be destroyed by the technology he has created, blundering into nuclear war or some irreversible ecological disaster, but also the threat that one of the products of that technology might supersede him. The computer poses such a threat, but at the same time it raises questions about man, his nature, priorities, capabilities and values, that could shake him out of his complacency and into a re-evaluation of his thinking, his purposes, his past and his projects.

The earlier discussions of the differences between the brain and the mind are resumed and developed with the help of the computer analogy. Bohm first brings it in, pointing out that the computer works on the basis of a programme which is put into it, and its operations depend upon its memory, so, 'therefore when we operate from memory we are not very different from a computer'. Krishnamurti seizes upon the analogy to remark: 'I would say that a Hindu has been programmed for the last 5000 years to be a Hindu; or, in this country, you have been programmed as British, or as a Catholic or a Protestant.' This programming, be it manifest in thought, feeling or conduct, is mediated by the brain, which 'lives entirely on the past, modifying itself with the present and going on'. The difference between the brain and the mind is that the brain is programmed but the mind is not. So long as the brain keeps running on its own, like a computer, its operations are ultimately meaningless. They may have practical uses and applications, but these functions can be far more competently performed by a computer.

So we have a situation in the world today which brings home what Krishnamurti had been saying for decades about the limitations of thought based upon time, memory, experience, and of any knowledge so gained. It is clear that if there is no interaction between the brain and the mind, and we just let the brain keep on running things, we are doomed. But 'contact can only exist between the mind and the brain when the brain is quiet'; then and only then can the brain's functions be governed not by thought, but by intelligence, awareness and insight. As we have seen, Krishnamurti maintained that insight can actually change the physical structure of the brain. If we have now been brought to the undeniable realization that our brains are nothing but second-rate computers, that change becomes all the more imperative.

Appendix

Bohm's *Wholeness and the Implicate Order*

Some parts of David Bohm's book, *Wholeness and the Implicate Order* have noteworthy correspondences with the themes of his discussions with Krishnamurti. It seems pertinent to conclude by drawing attention to these for, in so far as the book has had an influence within Bohm's professional sphere, it must have extended awareness of the relevance of Krishnamurti's philosophy.

It is clear from the dialogues that Bohm is no advocate of the materialist-mechanist world-view of conventional science. His book is an attempt to outline an alternative. Although he argues on a purely scientific basis that the conventional view, which involves analysing the world into independently existent parts, 'does not work very well in modern physics', the implications of the alternative he proposes extend far beyond the field of physics, and in the less technical chapters of the book he explores these implications. The basic point, though, is that science itself, on the basis of its experimental findings, has rendered the old view redundant and an alternative necessary:

> Relativity and quantum theory agree, in that they both imply a need to look at the world as an *undivided whole,* in which all parts of the universe, including the observer and his instruments, merge and unite in one totality.[42]

'Thought is the enemy,' said Krishnamurti, and Bohm points out how this has been the case in science. Thought divided things up for its own convenience, the better to comprehend and control them, but then it made the mistake of taking that fragmentation that it had projected upon the world as an inherent characteristic of the world itself. Because of the authority of science, this habit of regarding the world as a congeries of separate things became pervasive in all areas of thought, reinforcing the separatist and dangerously élitist tendencies of national, racial or class groups, supporting and justifying the rapacious exploitation of the natural environment, and resulting in man thinking about his own psyche in terms of its conflicting components. It may sound idealistic to demand a change in this ingrained habit of thought, but, Bohm argues, wholeness and the holistic world-view are not an ideal, they may well be the reality, as modern physics has shown. 'So what is needed,' he writes, 'is for man to give attention to his habit of fragmentary thought, to be aware of it, and thus bring it to an end.'

The principle of ending something through attention and awareness, rather than seeking to attain or superimpose its alternative, is of course the basic Krishnamurti strategy. For one world-view to contend with another, however right it may be, is still an operation in the field of thought, and, Bohm warns, we should beware of embracing the holistic view as a description of the world as it is, but should regard it rather as a theory which yields certain new insights. It is no good changing the content of our thought if our thinking processes don't change at the same time: 'Fragmentary content and fragmentary process have to come to an end *together*'. So our awareness has to be not only of what we think about the world but also of *how* we think about it, and the latter is the more difficult, for it is easier for us to accept that the outputs of our thinking processes may be fallible or provisional than that the processes themselves are. As Krishnamurti would have put it, both knowledge and thought must end for the mind to have insight into 'what is'. Bohm carries over into his own work this special connotation of the term 'insight'. He writes:

> To end this illusion [that the self and the world are broken into fragments] requires insight, not only into the world as a whole, but also into how the instrument of thought is working. Such insight implies an original and creative act of perception into all aspects of life ... [and] when such insight occurs, the source cannot be within ideas already contained in the field of measure but rather has to be in the immeasurable.[42]

In their very origins, Western and Eastern thought diverged, in that the former took 'the field of measure' (the reality that thought could encompass and systematize) as primary, whereas the latter regarded the immeasurable ('that which cannot be named, described or understood through any form of reason') as the fundamental reality. Their respective cultural biases, towards science and technology on the one hand and towards religion and philosophy on the other, were the outward manifestation of this divergence. In both cultures these biases became rigidified into traditions and dogmas, the West regarding the idea of anything beyond the field of measure as illusion, and the East likewise rejecting as *maya* everything within it. But in science the fundamental revolutionary insights have not come by way of progressive rational developments in the field of the known and measurable. In modern physics the field of measure itself has become so ambiguous and indeterminate that the very idea of a stable objective reality accessible to investigation has had to be abandoned. At the quantum level, the act of observation itself affects the phenomena observed, so any description has to include both the observer and the observed, and it has to be acknowledged that what is described is not something fixed and immutable but something abstracted from the universal flux, which is the field of the immeasurable. So Western science has had to recognize both the primacy of the field of the immeasurable as well as the inadequacy of its traditional methodology and logic to divine anything about that field.

Krishnamurti's insistence upon the poverty of thought and of the knowledge it engenders is thus vindicated by modern science. If the quantum world has yielded up some of its mysteries, it has only done so to minds that have shaken off their habitual thought-routines and become capable of a flash of perception. Following Krishnamurti, Bohm calls this flash 'intelligence' and speaks of it as endowed with energy. He also brings in the term 'the ground', though without the religious implications that it developed in the dialogues. He writes:

> If intelligence is to be an unconditioned act of perception, its ground cannot be in structures such as cells, molecules, atoms, elementary particles, etc. . . . The ground of intelligence must be in the undetermined and unknown flux, that is also the ground of all definable forms of matter.[42]

We recall Krishnamurti's saying that insight comes from the

universal Mind and that there is a 'something beyond' mind which is pure energy and is the ground of everything. In Bohm's formulation, this 'something beyond' is the universal flux, a totality which embraces mind and matter and within which everything is interconnected and interactive. To conceive of reality in terms of such a flowing movement of the whole, he maintains, is more consistent with the findings of quantum physics than to conceive of it in terms of the interaction of physical entities governed by mechanical laws. The latter view holds good in respect of many observed phenomena, and in the past has facilitated scientific discoveries, but at the quantum level of reality it breaks down; this partiality of the relevance of the physical laws that the mind can ascertain is to be expected because the limited mind cannot know the unlimited whole. That those laws apply and work within a specific order of reality is consistent with Bohm's theory that the universal flux is multidimensional, encompassing multiple orders of reality, each with its 'implicate' and 'explicate' content. The explicate order is the manifest, that which we apprehend with our conceptual and perceptual tools. The more subtle and sophisticated our concepts and perceptions are, the greater will be the content of the implicate order that becomes 'unfolded' into the explicate, or, to put it alternatively, the more meaning we shall be able to abstract from the universal flux.

Bohm is very conscious of how inadequate ordinary language is in these areas. He points out that in the phrase 'we abstract meaning' there is an implication of a dualism that is misleading. The subject-verb-object basic structure of our language derives from and reinforces the view that the world is made up of separate things, and we really need a new mode and structure of language (Bohm calls it the 'rheomode', i.e. 'flowing mode') to liberate language and thought from their bias towards the fragmentary world-view. He makes proposals for the creation of such a language, which will not be discussed here. Suffice it to note that ordinary language is a limited tool for investigating even 'the field of measure' (mathematical language is more sophisticated but still limited), but in respect of the immeasurable there is nothing it can say. As Krishnamurti put it: 'Explanations have been the boat to cross to the other shore. But there is no boat.'

In one of their last dialogues, Bohm asked Krishnamurti why, since it didn't seem to affect anybody, they should be doing what they were doing, and Krishnamurti answered, 'Because it is the right thing to do.' One can imagine that, with his reservations about the adequacy of the language he was using, Bohm might have had similar doubts about writing his book and might have allayed them with a similar answer. He modestly offers the book as a 'necessarily sketchy' investigation of 'the germ of a new notion of order': the order of 'undivided wholeness' in which the cosmos, matter, life and consciousness are seen as phenomena that derive from and will ultimately return to a common ground, the 'universal flux' of energy which is the ultimate 'implicate order' from which phenomena are continually 'explicated' or 'unfolded' in a process he terms 'the holomovement'. Sketchy though the investigation may be, it is firmly based upon the experimental and theoretical foundations of modern quantum physics. And in relating these to an overview consistent with, if not entirely derived from, Krishnamurti's teachings, Bohm has done much to 'relevate' those teachings (his own term, meaning 'to lift into attention again, to make relevant') and their implications to people who would probably not otherwise be acquainted with them.

Bibliography

Books by Krishnamurti:
1. *Early Writings*, Chetana, Bombay, 1969.
2. *The First and Last Freedom*, Gollancz, London, 1954.
3. *Commentaries on Living: First Series*, Gollancz, London, 1956.
4. *Commentaries on Living: Second Series*, Gollancz, London, 1959.
5. *Commentaries on Living: Third Series*, Gollancz, London, 1961.
6. *This Matter of Culture*, Gollancz, London, 1964.
7. *Freedom from the Known*, Gollancz, London, 1969.
8. *The Only Revolution*, Gollancz, London, 1970.
9. *Talks and Dialogues*, Avon Books, NY, 1970.
10. *The Urgency of Change*, Gollancz, London, 1971.
11. *The Impossible Question*, Gollancz, London, 1972.
12. *You are the World*, Harper and Row, NY, 1972.
13. *The Awakening of Intelligence*, Gollancz, London, 1973.
14. *Beginnings of Learning*, Gollancz, London, 1975.
15. *Tradition and Revolution*, Sangam Books, Madras, 1975.
16. *Krishnamurti's Notebook*, Gollancz, London, 1976.
17. *Truth and Actuality*, Gollancz, London, 1977.
18. *The Wholeness of Life*, Gollancz, London, 1978.
19. *Krishnamurti's Journal*, Gollancz, London, 1979.
20. *The Network of Thought*, Mirananda, Wassenaar, 1982.
21. *The Flame of Attention*, Mirananda, Wassenaar, 1983.
22. *The Ending of Time* (with David Bohm), Gollancz, London, 1985.
23. *The Future of Humanity* (with David Bohm), Mirananda, Wassenaar, 1986.
24. *Krishnamurti to Himself: His Last Journal*, Gollancz, London, 1987.
25. *The Future is Now*, Gollancz, London, 1988.
26. *Krishnamurti on Education*, Krishnamurti Foundation India, 1987.
27. *Washington DC Talks 1985*, Mirananda, Wassenaar, 1988.

Books and Essays on Krishnamurti:
28. Dhopeshwarkar, A. D., *Krishnamurti and the Experience of the Silent Mind*, Chetana, Bombay, 1956.
29. Dhopeshwarkar, A. D., *Krishnamurti and the Mind in Revolution*, Chetana, Bombay, 1971.

30. Goleman, Daniel, *Krishnamurti's Choiceless Awareness* (in Goleman, *The Varieties of Meditative Experience*, Dutton, NY, 1977).
31. Jayakar, Pupul, *Krishnamurti*, Harper and Row, NY, 1987.
32. Lutyens, Mary, *Krishnamurti: The Years of Awakening*, John Murray, London, 1975.
33. Lutyens, Mary, *Krishnamurti: The Years of Fulfilment*, John Murray, London, 1979.
34. Lutyens, Mary, *The Open Door*, John Murray, London, 1988.
35. Methorst-Kuiper, A. J. G., *Krishnamurti Chetana*, Bombay, 1971.
36. Needleman, Jacob, *A Note on Krishnamurti* (in Needleman, *The New Religions*, Doubleday, NY, 1970).
37. Niel, André, *Krishnamurti: The Man in Revolt*, Chetana, Bombay, 1957.
38. Suares, Carlo, *Krishnamurti and the Unity of Man*, Chetana, Bombay, 1953.
39. Tillett, Gregory, *The Elder Brother: A Biography of C. L. Leadbeater*, Routledge, London, 1982.
40. Vas, Luis (ed.) *The Mind of Krishnamurti*, Jaico Publishing House, Bombay, 1971.
41. Weeraperuma, Susanaga, *Living and Dying from Moment to Moment*, Chetana, Bombay, 1978.

Other books referred to in the text:

42. Bohm, David, *Wholeness and the Implicate Order*, Routledge, London, 1980.
43. Jaynes, Julian, *The Origin of Consciousness in the Breakdown of the Bicameral Mind*, Houghton Mifflin, Boston, 1976.
44. Koestler, Arthur, *Janus: A Summing Up*, Hutchinson, London, 1978.
45. Sheldrake, Rupert, *A New Science of Life*, Blond, London, 1980.

Index of Names and Places

Adyar 4, 17, 40
'Alcyone' 6, 7,
Aristotle, 143
Arundale, George 6
Auden, W. H. 104

Besant, Annie 4–9 *passim*, 13, 16, 17, 20, 21, 23, 55
Blake, William 44
Blavatsky, Helena 4, 5
Bohm, David 55, 121, 137–51 *passim*, 152–6
Bohr, Niels 137
Brockwood Park 35, 40, 41, 111
Bucke, R. M. 46
Buddha 12, 31, 33, 41, 51, 52, 75

Columbus, Christopher 54, 55
Crichlow, Keith 40

Dostoevsky, F. 61

Edison 54
Eerde, Castle 16, 18
Eliade, Mircea 11
Eliot, T. S. 1
Euhemeros 85

FBI 27
Freud, Sigmund 68, 69
Fromm, Erich 61

Gandhi, Indira 37–8
Gandhi, Mahatma 28, 29, 85

Grohe, Friedrich 40

Happy Valley School 28
Heisenberg, Werner 137
Huxley, Aldous 27, 28, 52, 66

James, William 71
Jayakar, Pupul 29, 30, 31, 36, 37, 38
Jaynes, Julian 140
Jesus Christ 4, 6, 14, 51, 81

Keats, John 35
Kierkegaard, S. 60, 82
Koestler, Arthur 140
Krishna, Sri 4
Krishnamurti Foundations 35, 40, 41, 51, 56, 57
Kuthumi, Master 5, 10, 11, 12, 80, 82

Leadbeater, Charles W. 4–10 *passim*, 13, 14, 20, 23, 49, 55, 80
Lutyens, Lady Emily 9, 13, 25, 50
Lutyens, Mary 13, 26, 50, 51, 55

Madanapalle 16, 28
Maharishi Mahesh Yogi 36
Maitreya, Lord 4, 5, 6, 12, 17, 18, 55, 80, 82
Mann, Thomas 26
Marx, Karl 60
Mehta, Nandini 30–1
Mill, J. S. 60
Mozart, W. A. 52, 53

Narianiah 5, 8
Nehru, Jawaharlal 28, 29, 30, 32, 37
Nityananda (Nitya) 5, 7, 8, 10, 11, 12, 14, 16, 17, 30, 135

Ojai 10, 11, 13, 16, 24, 27, 28, 30, 31, 34, 40, 41
Olcott, Col. 4
Ommen 16, 18, 19, 22, 24
Ootacamund ('Ooty') 30, 35
Order of the Star in the East (OSE) 6, 7, 8, 16, 17, 18, 21, 22, 24, 26, 122

Pallandt, Baron Philip van 16
Pauli, Wolfgang 137

Rajghat 28, 33, 41
Rajneesh, Sri 36
Rao, Shiva 17
Rishi Valley 28, 38
Roosevelt, President 27

Rousseau, J. J. 60

Saanen 34
Sartre, J. P. 60
Scavarelli, Vanda and Luigi 34, 35
Shakespeare, W. 35
Sheldrake, Rupert 54, 55

Tertullian 82
Theosophical Society 4, 17, 21

Warrington, A. P. 11, 12
Williams, Rosalind 11, 12
Wittgenstein, Ludwig 60
Wodehouse, P. G. 1
Wood, Ernest 5
Wordsworth, William 44

Yeats, W. B. 46

Zimbalist, Mary 39, 51, 55

Subject Index

action 88, 90, 94, 128
ambition 65
asceticism 87–8
attention 106, 108, 141–2
authority 62, 114
awareness 64, 73, 76

belief 81–2
'the benediction' 46, 47. 50
the brain 77, 141, 142

change 101, 104, 141
compassion 89, 149
competition 65, 114
the computer 39, 150–1
conditioning 62, 116
conflict 64–5, 87, 93–5, 111, 114
consciousness 71–2
creation/creativity 45–6, 70, 131, 148

death 64, 91, 97–8, 133
desire 64, 87, 88
discipline 87, 106
dualism 75, 93

education 110–20
energy 88, 103, 138–9, 142
evolution 139

fear 63, 75, 116–17, 129
freedom 60–7, 71, 107, 112

God 80, 82, 144
'the ground' 144–6, 148

happiness 72
human potentials movement 104, 106

insight 122, 138, 142–3, 146
intelligence 64, 78–9, 113, 116
the image 92, 105

knowledge 63, 78, 114, 139, 141
kundalini 13, 14

language 63, 86, 130, 155
learning 65, 114–5, 118
life 76, 91–6
love 67, 89, 92, 103–4, 105, 127, 129–30, 149

meditation 66, 72, 106–8, 148
memory 63, 77–8
mind 69–70, 142

order 79, 142
overcoming 131

pleasure 64, 95–6
poverty 102
problems 65, 73, 101, 121–35
'the process' 10–15, 30–2, 35, 51, 56, 77
psychoanalysis 68–9, 70

relationship 92, 102–3, 123, 127
religion 80–90, 136, 145
revolution 61, 65, 101

sacredness 85–6

security 91
the self 68, 73–6, 96, 98, 123, 127, 128, 140
self-awareness/knowledge 68, 125
self-improvement 65, 107, 149
sex 113, 131–2
shamanism 11
the silent mind 72–3, 77, 89. 148
suffering 75, 134, 149

Theosophy 4, 5, 6, 9, 21, 22, 23, 31, 49, 55, 81
thought 62–3, 76, 86, 92, 98, 139, 145
time 62, 63, 71–2, 98, 139
truth 80, 87, 105, 106

the unconscious 69–70, 73

violence 65, 150

wholeness 71, 88, 118, 152–3
the World Teacher 4, 6, 9, 16, 17, 19, 20, 23, 49, 50, 110
worship 84–5